Wealth of the Wilderness not o͏͏͏͏͏͏͏͏
but also into my own world ͏͏͏͏͏͏
into the wilderness rather than run from it has transformed the ways, rhythms, and practices of my life. I fear less; I courage more. *Wealth of the Wilderness* teaches us to not just endure wilderness seasons, but to flourish in and emerge from them as better creatures.

Kristi McLelland, professor at Williamson College;
founder and executive director,
New Lens Biblical Studies

Wealth of the Wilderness helped me identify the spiritual wilderness I had been in for a long time, embrace it, and allow God to transform me. It changed the way I interact with my husband and my kids. It changed the way I lead and do business. It changed me.

Suzanne Sims, senior executive vice president,
Ramsey Solutions

Journeying through *Wealth of the Wilderness* was transformational for me. Understanding the Bible through a Middle Eastern lens is truly life-changing—and addictive! The more I learn, the more I *want* to learn. I'll never view the wilderness seasons of life in the same way again.

Tamera Alexander, *USA Today* bestselling author

One must experience *Wealth of the Wilderness* to come out on the other side seeing the Bible and the wilderness through a new lens. By saying "yes" to journeying through *Wealth of the Wilderness* and allowing God to change you, the wilderness will become a place you long to be—not a place you avoid.

Tiffini Kilgore, founder, *The House of Belonging*;
author of *Misfit Table*

WEALTH of the WILDERNESS

To Krista —

Rebekah Joy

WEALTH of the WILDERNESS

A Middle Eastern Pathway for
Transformation through Difficult Seasons

REBEKAH JOY

MIDBAR PRESS

WEALTH of the WILDERNESS

Copyright © 2020 Rebekah Joy

Published in Nashville, Tennessee by Midbar Press

All rights reserved. No part of this publication may be reproduced, distributed, or transmitted in any form, or by any means, including photocopying, recording, or other electronic or mechanical methods, without the prior written permission of the author, except in the cases of brief quotations and certain other noncommercial uses permitted by copyright law.

ISBN: 978-1-7360705-1-2 (Softcover)

ISBN: 978-1-7360705-0-5 (eBook)

Unless otherwise indicated, Scripture quotations are from The Holy Bible, New International Version®, NIV® Copyright ©1973, 1978, 1984, 2011 by Biblica, Inc.® Used by permission. All rights reserved worldwide.

Scripture quotations marked AMPC are taken from the Amplified Bible, Classic Edition (AMPC) Copyright © 1954, 1958, 1962, 1964, 1965, 1987 by The Lockman Foundation.

Scripture quotations marked GW are taken from the GOD'S WORD Translation (GW) Copyright © 1995 by God's Word to the Nations. Used by permission of God's Word Mission Society.

Scripture quotations marked HCSB are taken from the Holman Christian Standard Bible®, Copyright © 1999, 2000, 2002, 2003, 2009 by Holman Bible Publishers. Used by permission. Holman Christian Standard Bible®, Holman CSB®, and HCSB® are federally registered trademarks of Holman Bible Publishers.

Scripture quotations marked KJV are taken from the King James Version.

Scripture quotations marked MSG are taken from The Message (MSG) Copyright © 1993, 2002, 2018 by Eugene H. Peterson.

Scripture quotations marked NASB are taken from the New American Standard Bible (NASB) Copyright © 1960, 1962, 1963, 1968, 1971, 1972, 1973, 1975, 1977, 1995 by The Lockman Foundation.

Scripture quotations marked NLT are from the New Living Translation, Copyright © 1996, 2004, 2007 by Tyndale House Foundation. Used by permission of Tyndale House Publishers, Inc., Carol Stream, Illinois 60188. All rights reserved.

Interior design and typeset by Katherine Lloyd, The DESK

Printed in the United States of America.

To all who
are wilderness weary.

CONTENTS

Preface... xi

Part 1
CHANGING THE WAY WE VIEW THE WILDERNESS

1 Which Lens Are You Looking Through?................3
2 What Is the Wilderness? 21

Part 2
TEN POSTURES FOR INHERITING WEALTH OF THE WILDERNESS

3   Engage the Process 33
4   Develop Eyes that See 47
5   Cultivate Ears that Hear 63
6   Express Authentic Emotions...........................75
7   Perceive Encounters with the Divine 85
8   Embrace the Becoming 97
9   Establish Healthy Rhythms 107
10 Make the Most of Delays and Detours................117
11 Embody the Wilderness...............................129
12 Emerge into a New Season...........................141

Acknowledgments..153
Glossary 155
Notes...157
Additional Resources 161
About the Cover 163

PREFACE

As I've been in the final stages of writing *Wealth of the Wilderness*, the world has been navigating a pandemic. The rapidly spreading COVID-19, also known as the novel *coronavirus*, has impacted humanity to a degree we've not experienced in recent decades. Quarantines and "safer at home" guidelines have been issued. School systems have moved to online. The food service industry has adapted to pick-up or delivery only, with some restaurants and businesses having to permanently close their doors. Economies have been hit hard as unemployment soars. Health care has been overrun.

Loss on all levels has been and is being felt. A people accustomed to coming and going as we like, we've experienced the loss of freedom to travel and move about. We've felt the loss of communal in-person gatherings for worship, concerts, and sporting events. We've lost jobs and income, as well as meaningful experiences such as senior proms and graduation ceremonies. We've experienced a loss of control—or, at least, the illusion of control—and most tragic, the loss of life.

I was scheduled to be in Egypt and Israel this month, exploring wilderness regions with a renowned Israeli desert archaeologist, as well as for further biblical studies in the land. But, as so many have experienced in recent days, my travel plans were interrupted because of the pandemic. All of us have been affected in some way.

One of the deepest fears we as humans experience is fear of the unknown. In her gripping memoir, *The Choice*, Holocaust survivor Dr. Edith Eva Eger relates the following exchange between she and a fellow prisoner, as they awaited their fate on a cold winter morning at Auschwitz:

"This line is death," the girl nearest me says. "This is the end." She is completely gray, as though she's covered in dust. Someone ahead of us is praying. In a place where the threat of death is constant, this moment still pierces me . . .

"We never know what the lines mean," I tell the girl nearest me. *What if the unknown could make us curious instead of gut us with fear?*[1] (emphasis added)

It's my hope that as you journey through *Wealth of the Wilderness*, whatever unknown you are facing . . . whatever wilderness terrain you are navigating, you'll experience a sense of calm assurance that you are being equipped to steward it effectively—positioned to receive *from* it and be transformed *through* it, instead of being passively impacted *by* it.

Thank you for allowing me to be your wilderness guide.

—Rebekah Joy
March 2020

Part 1

CHANGING THE WAY WE VIEW THE WILDERNESS

The desert was the place where the people would be alone with God. There, undistracted by the sight of natural or man-made beauty, they were hypersensitized to sound. They could hear the voice of God. . . . In the silence of the desert, the Israelites heard the Word and became people of the Word.

—Rabbi Jonathan Sacks

1

WHICH LENS ARE YOU LOOKING THROUGH?

> The Bible is an Eastern book. We see it through the colored glasses of Western culture. Much is lost . . . What lies between the lines, what is felt and not spoken, is of deepest significance.
> —Kenneth E. Bailey

I'll never forget the first time I stepped into the Judean wilderness of southern Israel. It was breathtaking. Beautiful. Majestic. Spacious. Vast, with no end in sight. Uniquely quiet and peaceful in the absence of city sounds. Rolling, rocky hills filled the rugged landscape as far as my eyes could see, with the occasional interruption of dark brown bushes—and one bright red desert flower amid it all.

I felt incredibly small among the seemingly endless wilderness hills and terrain. Small yet safe. Covered. Kept. Calm. In the right place, at the right moment.

Having joined up with a group of hikers, I stayed in proximity to them, yet far enough away to be able to take in my surroundings. Something was awakening deep in my soul. It would be years before I understood it, because in the moment I had no way of knowing what was on the horizon—transition and transformation through an eleven-year wilderness season.

I had moved to Bethlehem full of anticipation. The game of basketball provided my initial bridge to the land as I joined a club team in neighboring Beit Jala. I built relationships with Palestinians through working out at Bethlehem University, as well as through a community sports center where I volunteered and practiced with the men's basketball team.

The vast cultural differences between the Middle East and my Western way of living and understanding the world were quickly seen and felt:

In workout facilities, women exercised separately from men. Islamic women usually wore long-sleeved shirts and pants while exercising, along with a *hijab* or head covering.

Men rode through the streets in the backs of trucks, shooting firearms into the air and yelling. When I first encountered this, it wasn't until long after my heart rate had returned to normal that I learned it was done in a spirit of celebration.

Being multilingual was the norm, as personified by my landlord's twenty-one-year-old daughter, who was fluent in Hebrew, Arabic, German, French, and English. She began learning other languages in the first grade—a typical practice in her culture. As I embarked on the adventure of learning Arabic with my Palestinian tutor, the realization of how many languages my new friend could toggle back and forth between was quite inspiring.

There was no all-inclusive shopping supercenter in Bethlehem. It took me three weeks to locate clothes hangers in a store!

The five-time daily Islamic call to prayer, *adhan*, could be heard throughout the city via loudspeaker from one of many minarets built into mosques. Recited by the muezzin, the call summons Muslims to *salat*, or obligatory prayer. Devout Muslims would stop what they were doing, unroll their mats, and begin a series of prayers as they bowed in the direction of Mecca—birthplace of the prophet Muhammad.

Falafel, a Middle Eastern fast food, quickly became my favorite in the land. Made from ground chickpeas combined with herbs and spices, then shaped into balls or patties and deep-fried, falafel is often stuffed into a piece of freshly baked pita bread—which makes it even more delicious!

The people were kind, hardworking, hospitable, and always eager to help. It still brings a smile to my face thinking about multiple adventures riding on the back of a sport motorcycle through the streets of Bethlehem and Jerusalem, courtesy of my landlord's son. He demonstrated typical Middle Eastern hospitality in providing transportation for me when walking wasn't suitable.

Going through the Bethlehem checkpoint, I quickly learned the value of an American passport. I was repeatedly escorted to the front of a long line of Palestinians waiting to see if they would be admitted to the other side—perhaps to visit family in Jerusalem or to work outside the West Bank. I rarely experienced any delay, and I was never denied access. As I walked past businessmen and moms with rowdy children—all visibly weary of waiting, I was keenly aware of the stark difference in our realities and felt compassion toward them.

Bethlehem was and is a collision of archaic and modern, as demonstrated each time traffic stopped so a shepherd with flock of sheep in tow could safely cross the road.

Mindful of this traditionally modest culture, I wore long sleeves and pants in public, even in the one-hundred-degree weather with my primary mode of transportation being my feet. Taxis, or *sharees* in Arabic, were available; but within Bethlehem, most places were walkable, and I could learn the city better on foot.

I loved being in the land. The smells, the sounds, the simpler rhythms and way of life . . . I was finally home.

It seemed as if God had destined my heart to be connected to the Middle East, as my birth year, 1979, was a year of much movement in that region—so much so that 1979 has been called "the year that shaped the modern Middle East":

In February of that year, the last shah of Iran was overthrown during the Iranian Revolution, led by Ayatollah Khomeini. This uprising ended the Pahlavi dynasty and a twenty-five-hundred-year-old Persian monarchy. Later in '79, Khomeini founded the Islamic Republic of Iran and became its supreme leader.

In March, the Egyptian-Israeli peace treaty was signed by Anwar Sadat, president of Egypt, and Menachem Begin, prime minister of Israel. The signatures were witnessed by United States president Jimmy Carter.

Mid-July, Saddam Hussein, also known as the "Butcher of Baghdad," became president of Iraq.

On November 4, a group of Iranian college students took over the US embassy in Tehran; fifty-two American diplomats and citizens were held hostage for 444 days.

Late November, as nearly one hundred thousand people gathered for dawn prayer at the Grand Mosque at Mecca in Saudi Arabia, this holiest of Islamic sites was seized and held for two weeks by hundreds of Islamic extremists. These events are believed to have eventually given rise to al-Qaeda as they influenced the thinking of a wealthy young man named Osama bin Laden.

Late December, the Soviets invaded Afghanistan in what would become a nine-year war.

Interestingly, *Wealth of the Wilderness*—which provides a Middle Eastern view of wilderness—is being written in my fortieth year of life, coinciding with the fortieth anniversary of the year that shaped the modern Middle East.

My name is also a direct connection to this region. Biblical Rebekah, or *Rivkah* in Hebrew, was from the area of Haran in Upper Mesopotamia . . . modern-day Turkey. By marrying Isaac, son of the covenant, Rebekah joined Sarah in the Hebrew matriarchal line. She mothered Esau and Jacob, whose name God later changed to *Israel*.

Forms of Wilderness

Wilderness seasons often catch us off guard. Something happens, or doesn't happen, and we find ourselves thrust into a phase of life that stretches, refines, frightens, and ultimately changes us, depending on how we choose to steward it.

These seasons are subjective—what's wilderness for one person may not be wilderness for another, though there are some experiences we would likely all agree to be wilderness. The sudden death of a loved one. An unwelcome diagnosis. An unexpected loss, perhaps of a job, a friendship, or a marriage. An accident or tragedy that robs in such a way that we're left reeling, disillusioned and grief-stricken. When faced with such situations, words fail us. There's no possible way to understand or make sense in the moment.

Other circumstances are more *internal* wildernesses, such as perpetual anxiety or loneliness. Private realities magnified by fear of exposure or shaming. Mental illness or addiction experienced personally or within a family.

Some wilderness seasons are felt collectively, such as those times following acts of violence or natural disasters that rampage a family, city, or nation.

Oddly enough, there are other scenarios that may be desirable from the outside looking in, but for the one living through that season, it's a wilderness experience. For example, one person struggles to balance his fame, fortune, and influence with the loss of privacy and the weightiness of image management. Another is at the top of her game but wondering, *Is this it? Is this all there is?*

I live just outside Nashville, Tennessee. There's a lot of celebrity around here, and it's true: all that glitters is not gold. Listen to the lyrics of songs from any genre—you'll recognize words penned in and through wilderness. There is raw heartache behind the glamour.

Barrenness or wilderness of soul can happen simultaneously with outward flourishing, just as inner flourishing can occur during barren, wilderness seasons.

Wilderness comes in all forms and comes for us all.

Whatever the context of a wilderness season, one thing is certain: it marks us. It's as though we define our lives by pre- and post-moment or sequence of moments that led us into a wilderness. Life changes, which often changes us. That has certainly been true for me.

Dream Disrupted

After being in Bethlehem for a few months, I was in an internet café, checking my email, when my world suddenly shifted; I was returning to the States.

In a moment, my dream of living in the Holy Land for an extended season came to an abrupt halt. I had sold my car and left my job believing this new path was the direction I was headed. But now, as time seemed to stand still, all I could manage to think was, *what is happening?*

No longer could I anticipate the opportunity to learn conversational Arabic with a new Palestinian friend who wanted me to help her with her English. There was no more looking forward to my next basketball game or the women I would interact with as I volunteered at the community fitness center. The exhilaration of being able to explore the land as a resident instead of a tourist was unexpectedly gone.

Soon after receiving this news, I began the unwelcome journey back—which included a twelve-hour layover at an international airport. Disoriented and alone, I locked myself in a bathroom stall and wept uncontrollably; something within me felt like it had died.

Upon returning to the States, I experienced reverse culture shock. I struggled to reintegrate after having worked hard to adapt culturally to Middle Eastern surroundings. I remember moments when, without warning, I would smell the familiar aromas of falafel and fresh pita bread—as if I were walking the streets of Bethlehem. I couldn't quite get my heart and mind to be present with my physical body. I was incredibly lonely.

The sudden disruption of my dream seemed to yield loss after loss. Amid raw pain and manifold change, I could not yet comprehend all I was being positioned to inherit.

Walking the Path

Weathering a wilderness season can leave us solid, shaky, or perhaps some of both. How we emerge from that sacred space is determined by how we steward it.

No doubt you've seen glimpses of wilderness residue on people—perhaps it's even appeared on or in you. A new habit, hobby, or coping mechanism. A tattoo, piercing, or other symbolic addition. Deeper inner strength, resiliency, and empathy.

In the spring of 2007, as I hiked through the Judean wilderness, breathless with wonder, I didn't realize I was walking a tangible wilderness path I would soon be walking in extended fashion in my life.

As beautiful as the Judean wilderness was, there were also elements of danger. Moments when the path narrowed directly atop a cliff where one misstep could end in disaster. Getting lost if one strayed too far from the caravan of hikers. Dehydration from intense heat and sun exposure. Fatigue due to the length of the journey.

Awe and wonder. Real and imminent danger.

One hike with multiple potential outcomes, depending on how the path was walked.

Western Lens/Middle Eastern Lens

Wealth of the Wilderness is an invitation to embrace a *halakha*—Hebrew for "way of walking and living"—that positions us to inherit the riches available in wilderness seasons; riches that, to be received, may require modifying the lens through which we've been perceiving wilderness. When we do so, we may start to see, steward, and experience hard times in a whole new way.

I started wearing glasses as a six-year-old in the first grade. My new lenses helped me see more clearly and read without getting headaches. They enhanced my perception of the world around me and allowed me to see the blackboard without squinting.

My friend Kristi McLelland is the founder and executive director of New Lens Biblical Studies. As a biblical culturalist, teacher, and professor, she helps Westerners put on a new "lens"—a *Middle Eastern* lens—that positions us to view the Bible within its historical, geographical, cultural, and linguistic context.

We're going to do similarly during our journey together, as we look at wilderness through a new lens.

In *Reading the Bible with Rabbi Jesus*, author and teacher Lois Tverberg illustrates the vast distance between modern Western culture and that of the biblical world—which includes regions that are part of the modern-day Middle East:

> In our world, thin is beautiful.
>   In the biblical world, fat is blessing and wealth.
> In our world, youth is attractive.
>   In the biblical world, age is wisdom.
> Our world asks, *Does God exist?*
>   The biblical world asks, *Whose god is greatest?*
> Our world focuses on personal goals.
>   The biblical world focuses on family legacy.[1]

To help us establish a framework for our journey, let's discover some fundamental distinctions between Western and Middle Eastern cultures—understanding that cultural norms shape our mindset and actions. We'll refer to these generalizations or tendencies as *lenses* that will be anchor points of reference.

The chart below identifies these differences, which we elaborate on through the rest of the chapter.

Western Lens	Middle Eastern Lens
Form	Function
Individual	Communal
Innocence or Guilt	Honor or Shame
Understand then believe	Believe then understand
Acquire knowledge	Receive revelation
Abstract	Concrete
Destination	Journey
Entertainment	Hospitality

Form versus Function

In the West, we tend to focus more on the form of a thing. Middle Easterners focus on its function. For example, a Westerner might describe a car as "silver, with four doors and a sunroof"—detailing its *form*. In contrast, a Middle Easterner may say, "It has an engine built to last for years"—defining a car through the lens of *function*.

When I lived in Bethlehem, it was not uncommon to be walking down the street and see a BMW or Mercedes drive by, covered in mud. The car's appearance was not important; rather, it was the engine beneath the hood that mattered. The worth of the car was in its *function*.

Those same cars in Nashville are most often seen glistening with the afterglow of a fresh wash, free of anything that could cause them to look less than perfect. For Western cultures, *form*—how a thing looks—is valued over function.

When I visit various Middle Eastern cities, it's common to see piles of trash along the streets. Why? What's trash to one might be treasure to be repurposed by another. Tossing trash onto the street allows it to be readily accessible to whoever may need it. Function is key.

In a Western culture, trash goes in trash cans and is hauled away by trash crews. Littering is illegal; signs warn of fines for throwing trash on the street. Appearance, or form, is what matters most.

Individual versus Communal

One of the highest values for Westerners is individuality. This is seen in the drive to achieve personal status and establish a name for self, as well as through a sense of pride in doing it on one's own. "Me" over "we" is expressed in the ownership of personal property and a thriving industry centered around "self-help."

Lois Tverberg describes it like this: "What we [Americans] hear as children is, 'think for yourself' or 'stand on your own two feet.' Each one of us is responsible for his or her own success or failure. Indeed, we aren't seen as mature until we've 'left the nest' or 'cut the apron strings.'"[2]

Middle Easterners, on the other hand, value community and tribe. The success and wellbeing of the family or group is of utmost importance. Triumphs, failures, difficulties—even enemies—are shared. Multi-generational living among families is common, if not expected.

Tverberg continues: "In contrast, much of the world emphasizes just the opposite, knowing the advantages of functioning as a tightly knit team

... What children hear in collective cultures is, 'Welcome to the family! You belong! You're a member of a family, a tribe and a people. Together we will prosper! We are your team, your identity.'"[3]

In keeping with the individualistic mindset, Westerners approach learning through personal study and application.

Middle Easterners tap into the collective wisdom of their community to gain understanding about an idea. For example, the Jewish way of discovery, known as *yeshiva*, involves talking through a concept together to learn from the insight and experience of others.

When a Westerner meditates, the posture is one of quiet, private contemplation. In contrast, the Hebrew word for meditate, *hagah* (see Joshua 1:8), carries the idea of chewing on Scripture the way an animal passionately chews its prey.

Asking and responding to questions is a key aspect of communal dialogue. A wise rabbi once said: "We are closer to God when we are asking questions than when we think we have the answers."

Jesus modeled this when asked a question by His *talmidim* (disciples), the religious leaders, or the crowds who followed Him. He typically replied with a question or parable—rather than answering with a statement, as Westerners tend to do.

Innocence or Guilt versus Honor or Shame

Within the individualistic Western culture is an innocence-or-guilt paradigm. A person's actions are viewed as right or wrong. This is seen in Western justice systems, where an individual is tried and receives a guilty or not-guilty verdict from a judge.

The Middle Eastern, communal culture carries a deeply rooted code of honor/shame. Actions are perceived as being either honorable or shameful, which directly impacts the reputations of families and entire communities.

The honor/shame concept is exhibited through the still present-day reality of "honor killing." Also known as "shame killing," this practice involves the murder of a family member—typically a female—who is deemed to have committed an action that brings shame upon the rest of the family or community.

Actions, or the mere perception of dishonorable behavior, that may trigger an honor killing could include refusal to enter into an arranged marriage, having associations outside the community that are not approved of by the family—even being the *victim* of rape or sexual assault.

Honor killings are carried out to restore honor to the family or community. These acts may be performed publicly to serve as a warning to others within the tribe, should they be tempted to participate in the behavior regarded as dishonorable and shameful.

In describing this aspect of the Middle Eastern mindset, teacher Miriam Rodlyn Park adds: "Few things are worse than shame. It helps to explain honor killings; it doesn't justify them—the killings of women . . . acts of murder, for either real or perceived immorality . . . anything that would bring shame to her husband, her brothers, her family name."[4]

Jesus—a Middle Eastern rabbi—repeatedly rejected public humiliation and shaming. In one such scenario, His countercultural stance was visible through His interaction with the Samaritan woman at Jacob's well (see John 4:1–42). Westerners tend to view this passage through the innocence/guilt lens, perceiving Jesus to be calling out the woman's sin: living with a man, after being married to five previous men.

But when viewed through a Middle Eastern lens, Jesus was not naming her *sin*; rather, He was naming her *shame*. In a culture where only men could initiate and legally file for divorce, this woman had been divorced—or abandoned and rejected—by five different men. She was well acquainted with shame. Without the covering of a man, whether that be her husband, son, father, or brother, a woman was left vulnerable and unprotected.

In the gospel of John, Jesus burst through the cultural barriers of gender, class, and race. As a Jewish religious leader and teacher, He chose this ostracized, "half-breed" woman to be the first person, male or female, to whom He would explicitly reveal Himself as Messiah. In an honor/shame culture, Jesus was generously lifting her out of her shame and publicly restoring her honor.[5]

Here's what happened after their conversation:

Leaving her water jar, the woman went back to the town [Sychar, in Samaria] and said to the people, "Come, see a man who told me everything I ever did. Could this be the Messiah?" They came out of the town and made their way toward him . . .

Many of the Samaritans from that town believed in him because of the woman's testimony. (John 4:28-30, 39)

Being treated with dignity by Rabbi Jesus, instead of the disdain and shaming she had grown to expect, so impacted this woman that she immediately left to share the good news. The response of her fellow Samaritans, who had perhaps been the very ones shaming and disregarding her, is remarkable. The power of her testimony was irresistible.

Understand then Believe versus Believe then Understand

Westerners want to understand before they will believe, as exhibited in matters of faith. A Westerner often defines their faith by stating *what* they believe—as though their faith is a noun. They tend to ask questions fueled by the need to understand. The decision to believe or not believe directly hinges on whether they reach a point of understanding.

Middle Easterners choose to believe *before* they understand. To them, faith is a verb, and thus, belief is demonstrated by action. All throughout the Bible are stories of Middle Eastern men and women who believed God and proved their faith by taking Him at His word, even when the situations they were in were difficult, if not impossible, to understand.

Hebrews 11, often called the "Hall of Faith," highlights the faith of some by detailing how they *demonstrated* their faith rather than by stating *what* they believed:

By faith Noah . . . built an ark. (v. 7)

By faith Abraham . . . obeyed and went. (v. 8)

By faith Moses' parents hid him. (v. 23)

By faith the prostitute Rahab . . . welcomed the spies. (v. 31)

According to the *NIV First-Century Study Bible*, "Faith, particularly from a Jewish point of view, meant faithfulness, trust and insight. In Hebrews, faith is active and lived out rather than a matter of mere belief."[6]

Just over seven years into what would become an eleven-year wilderness season, God gave me eyes to see the area where I would eventually purchase a home. The *why* behind the location was clear, but the *how* didn't make sense, as at the time, I was not aware of any way it could happen. I didn't understand, but I chose to believe.

I demonstrated my belief by running and walking the streets of this area for several years, getting familiar with the surroundings. I looked at the homes, not knowing which of them was going to be mine but believing one of them was. I also talked with people who had connections in the area.

I now live in the location that was shown to me years earlier. Not because I understood how it was going to happen and then came up with a plan to bring it to pass. Rather, I believed and responded with action that kept me on the path of revelation becoming reality.

Knowledge versus Revelation

Western cultures have been strongly influenced by Alexander the Great and various Greek, or Hellenistic, philosophies. Knowledge is valued, and man is the measure of all things. Think Aristotle, Plato, and Socrates. The goal of study is to acquire more and more knowledge, often from a place of striving to obtain.

While the Greeks loved knowledge, the Hebrews—Jesus, Peter, and Paul—loved light. In the biblical world, there was an inherent posture of openness to hear and receive, as opposed to having to go find knowledge. And while Paul, for instance, was a highly studied rabbi, his underlying posture was not one of straining to know; rather, it was one of readiness to *inherit*. The apostle's wisdom and knowledge reflected the ongoing impact of revelation.

Abstract versus Concrete

Westerners tend to be more abstract in thought and expression, while Middle Easterners are concrete. In describing God, Westerners often use intangible terms, such as *loving, kind, merciful, compassionate*, and *faithful*—characteristics that cannot be physically seen or touched. Conversely, a Middle Easterner would describe God as a *shield*, a *fortress*, a *rock*, or a *shepherd*—concrete images that can be readily observed and experienced.

This cultural variance is evident in rabbinic teaching, which is entirely visual. If a disciple cannot see an object, a rabbi won't use it as an illustration. For instance, if a rabbi likens God to a rock, it's because rocks are visible to everyone listening. When Jesus taught, "The kingdom of heaven is like a mustard seed" (Matt. 13:31), there would likely have been mustard plants easily seen by all who could hear Him.

Destination versus Journey

In Western cultures, the goal is to reach a desired objective as quickly as possible. The most efficient way is the preferred way.

Westerners move toward their destination with a start-to-finish approach; time is viewed as linear. There's a beginning and an end. And while the goal of getting there fast may be achieved, maturation born over time is often forfeited.

Middle Easterners tend to value journey. They look back so they can move forward with greater insight. An example of this is a Hebrew principle called *remez*, meaning "hint." When Jewish people read Scripture, they ask, "What happened *here* before? What happened *like this* before?" Because the Bible is one Story, if something significant occurred in a specific location, they have an expectation of similar happening there again.

A quote from the late science fiction author Ursula K. Le Guin aptly sums up these cultural differences: "It is good to have an end to journey towards; but it is the journey that matters, in the end."[7]

Entertainment versus Hospitality

Before we move on, there's one more significant cultural difference to be emphasized: the West is a culture of entertainment, while the Middle East is a culture of hospitality.

Entertainment can yield passive spectators whose interests are catered to in some way. Again, think Alexander the Great, Athens and Greece, coliseums and amphitheaters. In modern Western culture, this would be the equivalent of movie theaters, sporting arenas, and concert stages.

Hospitality is the welcoming way of the Middle East, inviting strangers to pull up a chair and take a seat at the table, or relax under the covering of a tent. The Middle Easterner bids you to come as you are, inviting you in while drawing you out through conversation and story.

I've witnessed and been the recipient of Middle Eastern hospitality countless times. Numerous biblical studies' teams I've traveled with have shared a gracious Palestinian bus driver who demonstrates hospitality through his intentional care for us. After we visit Jacob's well in Nablus, he stops at a specific bakery to buy freshly made *kanafeh*—a sweet, cheesy dessert. Even though it can be purchased throughout the land, our bus driver says no one makes kanafeh as good as they do in Nablus, the city where it originated!

In *An Arabian Journey*, British explorer Levison Wood offers a fascinating account of his 5,000-mile trek around the Arabian peninsula, from Iraq to Lebanon. During those six adventure-filled months, Wood relied heavily upon Middle Eastern hospitality to survive and make it from one location to another. Regarding the necessity of this ancient practice, he says:

> The desert was a place where life must be lived to its fullest. As a result, the sands provided a sanctuary where unwritten rules directed the behavior of those who dared enter them. In a place so full of hardship, the principles of generosity and benevolence were omnipotent. Even a sworn enemy must be welcomed as a guest if he asked for hospitality, and treated as a member of the family.[8]

For a Middle Easterner, how they treat one in need of food, water, or shelter—whether they be friend or foe, is to their honor or shame. "Desert hospitality" is practiced throughout the biblical narrative, as we will soon discover.

The Hebrew word for "table" is *shulhan*, which is the equivalent of *sulha* in Arabic. According to Lois Tverberg, it "derives from the ancient belief that eating at the same table with others is the essence of a peaceful, harmonious relationship."⁹ This insight helps us better understand the actions described by David in Psalm 23: "You prepare a table [*shulhan*] before me in the presence of my enemies." A hospitable heart or culture can set a table of welcome most anywhere.

Wealth of the Wilderness is not intended to entertain. Rather, its essence is one of hospitality and invitation, welcoming you to lean in and engage—to be an active participant.

Wealth of the Wilderness is a transformational table. Stuff goes down at tables. Laughter. Tears. Storytelling. Revelry. Conversation. Restoration. Celebration. Remembering. And *transformation*.

At this table, you'll be positioned to encounter Jesus, the source of living water, who quenches thirst. The bread of life, who fills and sustains. A Galilean rabbi whose time in the wilderness yielded His *halakha*—His way of walking and living. (see John 4:10–14; 6:35)

The Judean hills I've mentioned . . . the ones that seized my heart years ago . . . they were Jesus' backdrop when He entered this world. According to Matthew 2, Jesus was born in Bethlehem in the region of Judea. God in human form first opened His eyes in a humble village believed by scholars to have had a few hundred occupants at most.

The source of living water, born in proximity to barren wilderness. The Bread of Life, born in Bethlehem or *Beit Lechem*—the House of Bread.

God knows how to set a table.

Psalm 78:19 says that during the Israelites' forty wilderness years, they questioned, "Can God really spread a table in the wilderness?"

Yes, He can.

Yes, He *did*.

God, who would later embody humanity as the source of living water, provided water in the wilderness as Moses struck the rock and streams flowed out.

God, who would take on human form as the Bread of Life, supplied bread from heaven in the wilderness, raining down manna for the people to eat.

He spread a table in the wilderness for the Israelites then. He is spreading a table in the wilderness for you now.

WHICH LENS ARE YOU LOOKING THROUGH?

Questions to Consider and *Yeshiva*

1. Are you currently in a wilderness season? If so, how would you describe your experience?

2. Take a few minutes to consider past wilderness seasons you have navigated. What were the circumstances? How did you feel throughout?

3. Refer to the Western Lens/Middle Eastern Lens chart on page 10. Which cultural tendencies do you see in yourself?

4. Is your current perspective of wilderness seasons focused on how quickly you can exit, or looking for what you can inherit in and through?

5. Do you tend to have more of a destination mindset or journey mindset?
   - Destination mindset thinks periodic; Journey mindset thinks ongoing.
   - Destination mindset plans to stop; Journey mindset plans to continue.
   - Destination mindset challenges you; Journey mindset changes you.
   - Destination mindset focuses on outcome; Journey mindset focuses on progress.

6. What words come to mind when you think about God being hospitable and setting a table for you in the wilderness?

2

WHAT IS THE WILDERNESS?

> The wilderness years were the time when the distance
> between heaven and earth was never shorter.
> —Rabbi Jonathan Sacks

I have a friend who served in the United States' military for nearly twenty years—including extensive time spent in various wilderness and desert locations.

As she recalls some of her adventures, she says that at times, her company traveled on the ground through a desert, and there would be nothing other than brown sand and rolling hills as far as the eye could see. The sun's reflection on the sand would cause optical illusions—the appearance of things that weren't there.

On other occasions, they would be driving and then suddenly come upon a group of trees that surrounded an oasis, or even a palace. Barren and lonely nothingness. Then, out of nowhere, a haven. A beautiful dwelling. Wealth *in* the wilderness. Reprieve *in* the desolate.

In fall of 2018, as I spent some time talking about the wilderness with world-renowned Israeli archaeologist, Holocaust survivor, and longtime Jerusalem resident Dr. Gabi Barkay, he warned of the various seasonal dangers of the wilderness.

In wintertime, he said, one must be aware of the potential for "sheet floods that come suddenly and are very strong." These "rivers in the desert" can be useful for Bedouins (nomadic desert dwellers) who divert the water and store it in cisterns, but deadly for the tourist hiker, who is unaware of signs foreshadowing a coming sheet flood.

In summertime, "the sun is sometimes crazy and cruel; radiation is stronger in the desert. Dehydration comes without warning and is deadly," so wilderness hikers must travel with plenty of water. Dr. Barkay alluded to the heat, drought, and lack of shade as "curses in the desert."

The best season to be in the wilderness, according to Dr. Barkay, is spring, when there is less likelihood of sheet floods, and temperatures are still mild in comparison.

While we can and should plan to enter a natural wilderness in optimal conditions, life circumstances rarely afford us the luxury of scheduling our entrance into a wilderness season. Therefore, it is vital that we understand how to position ourselves to receive from and be transformed through challenging times.

Reverse Claustrophobia

The first *Wealth of the Wilderness* "transformational table" I facilitated was a development opportunity for women who were stewarding influential platforms in various sectors—from nonprofit directors to executives in corporate America; church ministry leaders to musicians, teachers, and entrepreneurs.

One of these women was bestselling author Rebekah Lyons, who described wilderness in a way I'd not heard before, but her unique perspective has stayed with me. Rebekah said wilderness to her was like "reverse claustrophobia." Instead of being in a *confined* space, where she feels trapped, because the wilderness is so expansive...so wide-open and seemingly neverending, that, too, can make her feel as if there is no way out.

Betwixt and Between

What is this place and space called wilderness that simultaneously fills and empties, beckons and repels, strips and strengthens?

What Is the Wilderness?

Anthropologists Arnold van Gennep and Victor Turner developed two concepts that help us better understand the functions of wilderness. They describe one as a *rite of passage*—transitioning from one phase to another. And the other associated idea, *liminal space*, as "the place that is neither starting point nor destination but the place between."[1]

Author and Franciscan friar Richard Rohr describes liminal space as "an inner state and sometimes an outer situation where we can begin to think and act in new ways." He says, "We are betwixt and between, having left one room or stage of life but not yet entered the next." Rohr explains that "we usually enter liminal space when our former way of being is challenged or changed." He adds that "it is a graced time, but often does not feel 'graced' in any way. In such space, we are not certain or in control."[2]

Research professor and *New York Times* bestselling author Brené Brown's description of "the middle" enhances the idea of liminal space. She says: "The middle is messy but it's also where all the magic happens . . . all the tension that creates goodness and learning."[3]

Wilderness is the messy-but-magical middle. The in-between space positioning us for necessary transition and inviting us into transformation.

Form/Function of Wilderness

When looking at the wilderness through a Western lens, we might describe it as:

> barren and desolate
> hot and draining
> never-ending
> beautiful
> harsh
> quiet
> rocky
> sandy
> dangerous
> lonely and lifeless

. . . all descriptors of its *form*.

In contrast, viewing wilderness through a Middle Eastern lens shifts our perspective to see that it

> increases hunger and thirst
> heightens awareness
> provokes resistance
> requires surrender
> invites change
> summons courage
> prepares and equips
> exposes one's inner state
> stirs up healthy and unhealthy desires
> positions for undistracted encounter with God

. . . descriptions of its *function*.

Noun-Based versus Verb-Based

We've identified cultural differences between the West and the Middle East, with the variance between form and function being a primary emphasis throughout *Wealth of the Wilderness*.

As we also consider languages, an important distinction between Hebrew and English is that Hebrew is a verb-based language that focuses on *what* is being done, while English is noun-based, emphasizing *who* is doing it.

The biblical world and the present-day Middle East are verb-based or function-oriented cultures.

In *Walking in the Dust of Rabbi Jesus*, Lois Tverberg describes Hebrew as a "word-poor" language. She asserts that biblical Hebrew includes approximately 8,000 words, in contrast to more than 400,000 words in English. "Paradoxically," says Tverberg, "the richness of Hebrew comes from its poverty. Because this ancient language has so few words, each one is like an overstuffed suitcase, bulging with extra meanings that it must carry in order for the language to fully describe reality."[4]

In the chapters to come, as we discover ten postures that better position us to inherit wealth through our wilderness seasons:

WHAT IS THE WILDERNESS?

1. Engage the Process
2. Develop Eyes that See
3. Cultivate Ears that Hear
4. Express Authentic Emotions
5. Perceive Encounters with the Divine
6. Embrace the Becoming
7. Establish Healthy Rhythms
8. Make the Most of Delays and Detours
9. Embody the Wilderness
10. Emerge into a New Season

a unique Hebrew word will serve as the foundation for each posture. It will be important to keep Lois Tverberg's description of biblical Hebrew in mind as we unpack one or two meanings from these words that are like "overstuffed suitcases."

We will also want to be mindful of what these ten postures are *not*:

steps to finish before moving on to the next task.
a checklist guaranteeing a specific outcome when completed.

Bestselling author and international speaker Rob Bell addresses this propensity. He writes: "The impulse in our world when faced with tension is to come up with the seven steps or the formula so that if you do things in the right order the tension will go away. But that doesn't always work." Bell continues: "One of the marks of someone who has experienced significant growth in their soul is their ability to live in the midst of tension.[5]

The postures offered in *Wealth of the Wilderness* help us more effectively navigate the "tension" of wilderness seasons; they are ways of positioning ourselves—mindsets we can embrace and embody over time. Each posture begins with a *verb*, inviting us to be active, instead of passive, in and through our wilderness seasons.

Biblical Use of Wilderness

Wilderness regions are typically uncultivated, inhospitable, and uninhabited (other than Bedouin shepherds and families).

In the Bible, words translated as "wilderness," "desert," or "wasteland," occur nearly three hundred times, including terms such as *midbar, arabah, Negev,* and *eremos.*

Midbar

Midbar is the most used biblical term for *wilderness.* It means "uninhabited land." Those who live in the *midbar* are willing to relocate, and are often shepherds—as Exodus 3:1 says of Moses:

> Now Moses was tending the flock of Jethro his father-in-law, the priest of Midian, and he led the flock to the far side of the wilderness [*midbar*] and came to Horeb, the mountain of God.

The Israelites' forty-year wilderness journey occurred in various desert areas, including the Sinai:

> Exactly two months after the Israelites left Egypt, they arrived in the wilderness [*midbar*] of Sinai. (Ex. 19:1 NLT)

Arabah

Arabah describes steppe or desert plain regions. Arabah is ground dominated by salt, with little water and few plants.

Isaiah, an eighth-century BC Israelite prophet, used both *midbar* and *arabah* in the following passages:

> The desert and the parched land [*midbar*] will be glad; the wilderness [*arabah*] will rejoice and blossom . . . Water will gush forth in the wilderness [*midbar*] and streams in the desert [*arabah*]. (Is. 35:1, 6)

Negev

Covering a much smaller portion of land in biblical days than in the modern state of Israel, *Negev* means "dry" and is a rocky desert and semidesert region of southern Israel that surrounds Beersheba and Arad.

Averaging less than eight inches of rain per year, the Negev is intricately linked to the patriarchs: Abraham, Isaac, and Jacob. These seminomadic

Hebrews grazed their livestock in the Negev desert area during the winter. In the summer months, they journeyed north to the hill country of Judah, near Bethel and Shechem.[6]

The book of Genesis repeatedly references the patriarchal connection to the Negev.

Then Abram set out and continued toward the Negev. (12:9)

Abram went up from Egypt to the Negev, with his wife and everything he had... From the Negev he went from place to place until he came to Bethel. (13:1, 3)

Now Abraham moved on from there into the region of the Negev and lived between Kadesh and Shur. (20:1)

Now Isaac had come from Beer Lahai Roi, for he was living in the Negev... From there he went up to Beersheba [in the Negev desert of southern Israel]. (24:62; 26:23)

Jacob left Beersheba [in the Negev] and set out for Harran. (28:10)

So Israel [Jacob] set out with all that was his, and when he reached Beersheba [in the Negev], he offered sacrifices to the God of his father Isaac. (46:1)

Eremos

In the New Testament, which was written in a form of Greek, the word most often used for wilderness regions is *eremos*—meaning "isolated, lonely, or desolate."

Eremos is sometimes combined with *topos*, Greek for "place," as seen in Mark 1:

Before daybreak the next morning, Jesus got up and went out to an isolated place [*eremos topos*] to pray. (v. 35 NLT)

Wilderness as the Backdrop

Wilderness, or *midbar*, is an underlying theme throughout the biblical narrative.

Torah, the first five books of *Tanakh*—also known as the Hebrew Bible or the Christian Old Testament, was given in the wilderness.

The *mitzvot,* or 613 commandments—including the Ten Commandments, were received at Mount Sinai in the wilderness.

Once a year on *Yom Kippur,* the Day of Atonement, the High Priest would lay hands on the head of a live goat while confessing the sins of the people of Israel. This "scapegoat" would then be sent away into the wilderness, symbolizing the removal of the people's sins.

Shepherds, prophets, kings, rabbis, and apostles; Moses, Elijah, David, John the Baptist, Jesus, and Paul. All had significant wilderness experiences, as did Hagar, an often-overlooked Egyptian maidservant.

Herod the Great, ruler of Judea when Jesus was born in Bethlehem, built at least two of his palace fortresses—Masada and Herodium—in the Judean wilderness.

The wilderness has a distinct ambiance; it is the ideal setting for necessary change. Chief Rabbi Lord Jonathan Sacks describes it as "a no-man's land" with "no settled population, no cities, no civilisational order."[7]

For the Israelites post-exodus from Egypt, the emptiness of the wilderness positioned them to be alone with God and one another. In that desolate place, they could embrace a new identity and experience rebirth as servants of the living God, no longer slaves to Pharaoh.

The wilderness beckons the lofty and lowly, rich and poor, lovers of God and lovers of self. There is no other place or space on earth like it.

In *The Gifts of the Jews*, scholar Thomas Cahill paints a vivid picture of why the rugged, uncivilized desert was the necessary context for the Israelites to encounter the living God as they did. For God to speak to and be heard by them, "it could happen only in a place stripped of all cultural reference points, where even nature seemed absent," says Cahill. "Only amid inhuman rock and dust could this fallible collection of human beings imagine becoming human in a new way. Only under a sun without pity, on a mountain devoid of life, could the living God break through the cultural filters that normally protect us from him."[8]

Sometimes it takes a setting void of the comforts we naturally reach for, or the distractions we don't even realize are diverting our attention, to afford us the opportunity to know God and ourselves in ways that lead to transformation.

Eat the Mystery

Every day for forty years, God supplied bread from heaven for the children of Israel as they journeyed through the wilderness. Unfamiliar with this edible substance, the Israelites called the bread *manna*, which sounds like the Hebrew for "What is it?"

Though the Israelites didn't understand exactly what manna was, they believed it to be provision from the right hand of God—and by faith, they *ate the mystery* in the wilderness.

As you journey through your wilderness seasons, you too are being invited to eat the mystery. *Mystery* implies it won't always make sense. There will be uncertainties and unknowns.

When you don't understand, will you choose to believe?

When you want to run from, will you take courage and move toward God?

When you're tempted to strive and strain, will you adopt a posture of receiving?

Provision and life are found in the mystery.

As you take your seat at this transformational table, will you do as the Israelites did and *eat the mystery*?

Questions to Consider and *Yeshiva*

1. Revisit the "Form/Function of Wilderness" section on pages 23–24. Which descriptors of wilderness most resonate with you at this stage in your journey?

2. If wilderness plays such a significant role in God's transformative work in us, what hinders us from weathering and walking wilderness seasons well?

3. How does the reality of the wilderness theme throughout the biblical narrative cause you to perceive wilderness seasons differently?

4. In what ways is it a challenge for you to "eat the mystery" of wilderness . . . to settle into the uncertainty that comes with it?

Part 2

TEN POSTURES FOR INHERITING WEALTH OF THE WILDERNESS

Life's difficulties do not allow us to stay the same. They move us. The question is, in which direction will we be moved: forward or backward?

—John C. Maxwell

3

ENGAGE THE PROCESS

> There is no shortcut to liberty.
> —Rabbi Jonathan Sacks

As has been mentioned, a Middle Eastern lens focuses more on the journey than the destination. For the inherent wealth of wilderness seasons to be discovered and inherited, we must look through the lens of journey and choose to *engage the process*.

Halakha

Halakh is a Hebrew word meaning "to walk." *Halakha* is "a way of walking or living." For the Hebrews, how they chose to live their lives, the way they purposely elected to walk, was their *halakha*.

The prophet Isaiah spoke about walking:

> Many peoples will come and say, "Come, let us go up to the mountain of the Lord, to the temple of the God of Jacob. He will teach us his ways, so that we may walk [*halakh*] in his paths." (2:3)

> Whether you turn to the right or to the left, your ears will hear a voice behind you, saying, "This is the way; walk [*halakh*] in it." (30:21)

In an interview with Dr. Miroslav Volf, founder and director of the Yale Center for Faith and Culture, Rabbi Jonathan Sacks describes the Jewish mindset by saying: "The life worth living in Judaism is a journey;

it's not a state of being. Judaism is about walking, about the way, about following the call of God."[1]

This Middle Eastern mindset of movement and journey is also evident through the Arabic term *sharia*. The late apologist Nabeel Qureshi refers to a religious teacher who explained *sharia* as meaning "the path;" specifically, the "correct path we must walk according to Allah's will."[2]

As we become acquainted with this first posture, *engage the process*, the question for us to wrestle with is, *Are we willing to* halakh, *or walk, the path before us?*

At the end of *The Lion, the Witch and the Wardrobe*, book one in C. S. Lewis's Chronicles of Narnia series, Queen Susan courageously declares: "Let us go on and take the adventure that shall fall to us."[3] Wilderness, whenever and however it comes, is an invitation to say "yes" to the adventure that has found us . . . as painful, inconvenient, or stretching as it may be.

Leadership expert John Maxwell offers this challenging statement: "Pain prompts us to face who we are and where we are. What we do with that experience defines who we become."[4]

Though we seldom decide on the timing and type of wilderness, we always get to choose how we will walk out wilderness seasons. We choose our *halakha*, which begins with the decision to engage the process.

Will we be passive spectators or active participants? The latter positions us for transformation through the wilderness.

Will we go through the wilderness or grow through it? Going through the wilderness with a *How much longer?* or just-getting-by mentality may prevent the very transformation we are being invited into.

Will we survive it and **thrive in it?** When our *halakha* is postured toward thriving, even during extremely difficult times, when survival is the sole objective, we tend to find a way to thrive in it.

Will we conform or be transformed? Conformity allows us to blend in and be like everyone else. It can keep us from taking personal responsibility. Transformation is a deep, individual work that no one can do for us.

Will we resist or yield? There is something to giving in . . . saying yes even when we don't understand or agree. A *halakha* of yielding keeps us open to being transformed, while resisting often prolongs the very challenge we are battling.

A Transformational Journey

To engage the process, we've got to shift our focus from a start-to-finish destination mindset. We are choosing to look through the lens of journey, accepting the reality that transformation takes time.

Geographically speaking, it's not far from Egypt to the Promised Land. But as is so often the case, the journey takes longer than we anticipate and requires more than we knew we had to give. The recently freed Israelites weren't merely embarking on a trek through the wilderness. Rather, their journey was holistic; a transformational process that impacted more than just their physical bodies.[5]

When I hike through Israel's Wilderness of Zin with a team of pilgrims, each of us must choose to walk the dusty, rocky, sometimes steep path before us. While we certainly help and encourage each other along the way, no one can walk the path for another.

When we reach the end, emerging from Zin hot, sweaty, and the best kind of tired, there is a triumphant sense of accomplishment at having chosen to brave the arduous path. Hikers often feel deep internal movement—even if there are not a lot of words to explain it in the moment.

Team members have summed up their experience hiking through and out of Zin as

> amazing
> life-changing
> baggage-dropping
> unbelievable
> beautiful
> shedding

One even said, "It left me speechless."

Transformation happens in and through the wilderness when our *halakha* includes a willingness to walk the path before us.

Functions of Wilderness

As we approach wilderness by uncovering its function, we'll be able to better comprehend the biblical storyline, much of which is set within a wilderness context. It will also position us to establish our *halakha* and determine if we are willing to engage the process necessary for receiving wealth from our wilderness.

As the following wilderness scenarios are introduced, consider what you are noticing in them about the functions of wilderness. We'll dive deeper into some of these narratives in future chapters—discovering the *halakha* of the men and women involved as they journeyed in and through the wilderness.

Hagar

From the beginning, the odds were against Hagar.

> In a patriarchal culture, she was a female.
> In a Hebrew household, she was an Egyptian.
> In a wealthy family, she was poor.
> In a free home, she was a servant.

As was culturally common in her day, Hagar was forced to sleep with her mistress's husband, Abram, because his wife, Sarai, had not been able to conceive. In a day and time when a woman's worth was determined by her womb—her ability to produce offspring to continue the family line—pressure was mounting for Sarai. And this was no ordinary Middle Eastern family. God had promised Abram that he would become a great nation (see Gen. 12:1–3; 15:4–5), yet Abram had no descendants . . . and both he and Sarai were advanced in years.

Upon learning that she was pregnant, Hagar treated her mistress Sarai with contempt. If we view the world through her paradigm, her actions become more understandable. This may have been the first time Hagar had ever felt her own sense of value. In getting pregnant, she had been able to do something Sarai, the Hebrew wife of wealthy Abram, had not.

Sarai, dealing with her own insecurity, fear, and frustration, so abused Hagar that the maidservant fled to the wilderness. There the angel of the Lord found Hagar by a spring of water on the road to Shur.

What happened after the angel found Hagar in the wilderness? How did this wilderness encounter shape the rest of Hagar's life?

We'll think about these questions as we take a much closer look at this more-than-meets-the-eye Egyptian maidservant who experienced the wilderness as a place of escape and encounter.

Moses

Moses had the world at his fingertips. Having been raised in the Egyptian Pharaoh's palace, whatever this adopted Hebrew desired was within reach. He was *royalty* inside the Pharaonic house.

Until.

When Moses came across an Egyptian who had been beating one of his fellow Hebrews, he took justice into his own hands and killed the Egyptian. Soon after, Pharaoh heard about it and tried to kill Moses.

The onetime prince of Egypt fled to Midian, wilderness region in northwestern Arabia, seeking sanctuary from the fallout of his own destructive choices.

How did God meet Moses in the wilderness, even though Moses fled there to escape the mess he had gotten himself into? What did forty years in the wilderness cultivate in Moses that the luxuries of Pharaoh's palace could have never afforded him?

Through the experiences of this mighty prophet and future deliverer of the Israelites, we will glean much about the wilderness as a place of shelter and preparation.

Elijah

A prophet and miracle worker living in the northern kingdom of Israel during the reign of King Ahab, Elijah embodied the meaning of his name: *My God is Yahweh*. His confident representation of the living God was on display at Mount Carmel, as Elijah stood alone against 450 prophets of the pagan god Baal, and 400 prophets of the false goddess Asherah.

Though Ahab was king, Jezebel ruled the kingdom. This former Phoenician princess—whose name has come to symbolize evil, cruelty, and immorality—influenced and infiltrated the northern ten tribes with the worship of Baal, god of the Phoenicians. After Elijah called down fire from heaven, besting the prophets of Baal and having them all killed, the enraged, revenge-seeking Jezebel issued a 24-hour death warrant on Elijah's life.

Having just experienced the power of the Lord in a most dramatic, public fashion, Elijah fled, terrified. Leaving his servant in Beersheba, Elijah continued into the wilderness, a region described as "dangerous and foreboding."[6]

Why would a mighty prophet who had been a supernatural conduit of God's miraculous power run into the wilderness? How long did he stay, and what happened while he was there?

As we will discover, Elijah's flight to the wilderness was intentional; he was headed to a specific location. The wilderness not only provided distance from those who sought to kill him, but it was an avenue of divine encounter and deep emotional expression.

David

The future king of Israel, David, a shepherd-turned-mighty-warrior from Bethlehem, was being pursued by King Saul, who currently occupied the throne and wasn't about to let this upstart take over. Saul's intense jealousy fueled his desire to kill David.

First Samuel 23 details David on the run from Saul, hiding in wilderness strongholds and hills throughout the Desert of Ziph and the Desert of Maon.

Though Saul searched relentlessly for David, God didn't give David into Saul's hands. The wilderness was a place of sanctuary and refuge for David and his men, a natural fortress offering protection and covering.

We'll take a closer look at the work the wilderness did in David the shepherd-king . . . and how the *absence* of wilderness experience deeply impacted his son Solomon, the third king of Israel.

The Israelites

The Israelites were escaping Pharaoh, Egypt, and 430 years of oppression. In Exodus 13, we learn that God intentionally led them through the wilderness, instead of taking them the shorter route through Philistine territory. As we'll discuss more later, God did this as a form of protection. Having only recently been freed, the Israelites were not in a position to fight. God was keeping them from being tempted to return to Egypt.

God provided space and place for the Israelites to exchange their slave mentality for the mentality of free people—a transformation so intense it would require the next generation, born into freedom instead of slavery, to make the transition.

The chart below helps us better understand the mental shift God was inviting the Israelites into.

Mentality of a Slave	Mentality of a Free Person
Strive and strain to get	Posture to receive
Fear and scarcity	Assurance and abundance
"Tell me what to do."	"Teach me how to live."
Blame others	Take personal responsibility
"It will always be this way."	"How can I make it better?"

Thomas Cahill gives us insight into the severity of the Sinai desert into which the Israelites were led post-exodus, after crossing the Red Sea (or the "Sea of Reeds" as it is more accurately translated). He describes the Sinai as "one of our planet's most desolate places." Cahill says it would be "hard to conjure up a landscape more likely to lead to death—a land bereft of all comfort, an earth of so few trees and plants that one may walk for hours without seeing a wisp of green, a place so dry that the uninitiated may die in no time." However, Cahill continues, "this desert brings not death but epiphany, the wildest, most exhausting, most terrifying epiphany of the whole Bible."[7]

The wilderness invited a type of deep internal work in the Israelites that could not come through any other avenue. The dry and dusty desert was the conduit for necessary change.

John the Baptist

Fiery and passionate, John the Baptist was cousin to and forerunner of Jesus, as foretold by the prophet Isaiah: "A voice of one calling: 'In the wilderness prepare the way for the Lord; make straight in the desert a highway for our God'" (40:3).

Referring to John, Luke 1:80 says, "The child grew and became strong in spirit; and he lived in the wilderness until he appeared publicly to Israel." Readying the way for Jesus, John the Baptist proclaimed a message that had been formed and fashioned in him through thirty years of private preparation as he was hidden in the hills of the Judean wilderness. As John preached in the wilderness, the Judeans and people of Jerusalem went out to hear him and be baptized in the Jordan River.

Why did it take so many years in the wilderness to ready John for his role as one who paved the way for Jesus? What about John's message and essence drew crowds to come hear him *in the wilderness*?

John received the greatest compliment Scripture records being given by Jesus. He said: "'I tell you the truth, of all who have ever lived, none is greater than John the Baptist'" (Matt. 11:11 NLT).

Years of preparation in the wilderness shaped a man who was spoken of more highly by Jesus than any other human being before or after.

Jesus

As was customary, Jesus was thirty years old when He received His rabbinic authority by being baptized in the presence of three witnesses: John the Baptist, God the Father, and the Holy Spirit. After He emerged from the waters, the Spirit led Him into the wilderness.

Why would the wilderness have been a fitting post-baptism experience for Jesus? What might He have expected the wilderness testing to do in and for Him?

The wilderness was a time of preparation for Jesus, with His most challenging test still on the horizon.

Paul

A zealous persecutor of Christians, Saul of Tarsus encountered the resurrected Jesus on the road to Damascus. Following that eye-opening experience, Saul, who would come to be known as the apostle Paul, did not immediately seek out interaction with the more experienced disciples and apostles—though that would have been a natural next step.

Instead, he headed to the Arabian desert—believed by most scholars to be Petra, in modern-day Jordan—for three years.

Though details are not given regarding Paul's wilderness years, the rare perseverance he carried (see 2 Cor. 11:23-27) reflects the desert deposits he received in Arabia. The in-between space no doubt played a part in his transformation from persecutor of Christians, to a man with such deep internal conviction that he would eventually *be* the persecuted Christian, being beheaded by the Romans under Nero's rule.

The Essenes

Have you ever wondered about the blank page in between the Old and New Testaments in some Bibles? That empty, white page seems to communicate that nothing happened during the four-hundred-year window often referred to as the "silent years." Though there were no Israelite prophets and no active writing of biblical books during that time, those years were anything but silent.

This time frame is known as *the intertestamental period*, during which Alexander the Great sought to influence and take over the Hebraic customs and values with his knowledge-esteeming, entertainment-driven Hellenistic (Greek) culture. Hellenism can be summed up like this: *If it tastes good, eat it. If it feels good, do it. If it looks good, watch it.*[8] The Greeks' overt lack of restraint would have been culture shock for the Hebrews.

Beth Shan, also known as Scythopolis, was part of the Decapolis (ten-cities region) during Jesus' time. The impressive ruins of this city reflect its Hellenistic influence. Each time I visit, I am sobered by the reality of all that went on there. Even the latrine, or public bathhouse, was designed around entertainment. With a stage at the center, patrons could watch and listen to performances—*while* relieving themselves.

This was a world obsessed with entertainment and self-gratification. This was also the world Jesus sent His disciples into.

Amid all this, three sects of Jews—the Pharisees, Sadducees, and

Essenes—rose up to combat Hellenism as they sought to maintain the Jewish way of life.

The Pharisees were common, blue-collar men who hated Rome and were loved by the people. They oversaw the local synagogue and were teachers of the law. There were around six thousand Pharisees.

The Sadducees were wealthy aristocrats sympathetic to Rome and hated by the people. They oversaw the temple and lived in Jerusalem. The Sanhedrin court, made up of seventy-plus-one Sadducees, has been described as having the combined power of Wall Street (financial) *and* the Supreme Court (legislative) *and* the Vatican (religious).[9]

Our focus is on the Essenes, separatist priests and devout Jewish men who refused to conform to Hellenism and the influence of Alexander the Great. They relocated to the desert to live an ascetic life in the caves around Qumran, an ancient Jewish settlement on the shores of the Dead Sea.

Between two thousand and three thousand Essenes lived communally in that desert region, choosing to relinquish personal property and money. The Essenes practiced a life of piety, strict observance of Sabbath, and commitment to studying the Scriptures. They functioned as scribes and are well-known for their connection to the Dead Sea Scrolls, considered the most important archaeological find of the twentieth century.

When going through the Israel Museum, I am always fascinated by the Qumran/Dead Sea Scrolls exhibit. This display includes excerpts from the Essenes' Rule of the Community, previously called the "Manual of Discipline," which was one of the first scrolls to be discovered at Qumran in 1947.

In describing the purpose of the Essenes' desert lifestyle, one passage says: "They shall separate from the habitation of unjust men and shall go into the wilderness to prepare there the way of Him [God]."[10]

In *The Jewish War*, written around AD 75, Josephus, a first-century Roman-Jewish historian, wrote: "The Essenes prefer a severer discipline. . . They eschew pleasure-seeking as a vice and regard temperance and mastery of the passions as a special virtue."[11]

Inspired by Isaiah 40:3, which we viewed in regard to the coming of John the Baptist, the Essenes chose a communal, simplistic, and purist life when conformity was becoming the norm under the influence of Alexander the Great.

The late apologist Ravi Zacharias said: "The Hebrews pursued light as an ideal; the Greeks pursued knowledge as the ideal; and the Romans pursued glory."[12] As lovers of light, these Jewish men were fervent in their desire to preserve the Hebrew way of life from Greek infiltration.

Each time I walk through Qumran, viewing remnants of the Essenes' scriptorium, Jewish ritual baths, and caves in the desert cliffs—all set against the backdrop of the Judean wilderness, there is a sense of the consecrated, set-apart nature of this unique community. Extreme as some of their practices may have been, the Essenes opted to live counterculturally by running *from* the world *into* the desert.

The Desert Fathers and Mothers

Beginning in the third century AD, the Desert Fathers and Mothers continued this pursuit of transformation and nonconformity.

When persecution and martyrdom under Nero ceased and Constantine made it acceptable for Christians to worship by declaring religious tolerance for them throughout the Roman Empire, a group of devout men and women headed to the Egyptian desert. This bold move countered what would have been a more typical response to their newfound acceptance: relief, gratitude, and anticipation of a life no longer shrouded by fear and risk.

Referring to the actions of these deeply committed believers, Henri Nouwen, a theologian and Dutch Catholic priest, said: "If the world was no longer the enemy of the Christian, then the Christian had to become the enemy of the dark world. The flight to the desert was the way to escape a tempting conformity to the world."[13]

In *The Wisdom of the Desert*, Thomas Merton, an American Trappist monk, theologian, and mystic, wrote: "Society . . . was regarded [by the Desert Fathers] as a shipwreck from which each single individual man had to swim for his life." Merton continues: "These were men who believed that to let oneself drift along, passively accepting the tenets and values of what they knew as society, was purely and simply a disaster."[14]

Describing the response of Saint Anthony of Egypt and his fellow monks, Nouwen said: "They escaped from the sinking ship and swam for their lives. And the place of salvation is called desert."[15]

Athanasius of Alexandria referred to the desert as having become a city, after thousands fled there to pursue a life of discomfort and sacrifice.

Why Wilderness?

Hagar fled relational turmoil.
Moses fled his poor choices.
Elijah fled a death threat.
David fled his pursuers.
The children of Israel were led.
John the Baptist embodied.
Jesus was compelled.
Paul prepared.
The Essenes resisted and abstained.
The Desert Fathers and Mothers ran from by running to.

Why did an Egyptian maidservant, a Hebrew-turned-Egyptian-prince, a mighty prophet, and a future king all *run to* the wilderness?

Why would God lead a nation out of captivity *through* the wilderness?

What was the Holy Spirit doing by *sending* Jesus into the wilderness?

What role did the wilderness play in helping our spiritual ancestors *resist* immorality and illicit forms of pleasure?

What made men and women free from the threat of persecution and martyrdom, *choose* to exchange their newfound physical safety for a life of restraint in the desert?

The answers are found in the *function* of wilderness. It was a place of

refuge . . . sanctuary . . . escape
transition and transformation
preparation . . . provision . . . encounter

Hagar the Egyptian, the Hebrews, and the Desert Fathers and Mothers moved *toward* the wilderness, not away from it, because they seemed to have an innate understanding of what they might experience there.

ENGAGE THE PROCESS

As we move forward, the next three postures are related to our senses of seeing, hearing, and feeling. The in-between space of wilderness uniquely positions us to have each of these senses heightened. By choosing to *engage the process*, we become increasingly aware of this opportunity, and are more prone to take advantage of the growth it offers.

Questions to Consider and *Yeshiva*

1. If you are presently in a wilderness season, do you see yourself as
   - passive spectator or active participant?
   - going through or growing through?
   - surviving and thriving?
   - being conformed or transformed?
   - resisting or yielding?
   - a combination of all, depending on the moment?

2. What adjustments will you make to your *halakha*—your way of walking and living wilderness seasons?

3. Do you agree or disagree that wilderness is an adventure that finds you? If so, what has this looked like in your life?

4. Refer to the functions of wilderness noted on page 44. Which of these have you experienced through your wilderness seasons? How so?

4

DEVELOP EYES THAT SEE

> Earth's crammed with heaven,
> And every common bush afire with God;
> But only he who sees takes off his shoes;
> The rest sit round it and pluck blackberries.
> —Elizabeth Barrett Browning

We have established that a Western lens views an object by its form, how it looks or appears, while a Middle Eastern lens focuses on function, what it does.

As we *develop eyes that see*—the second *Wealth of the Wilderness* posture—understanding the form-versus-function cultural difference anchors us in knowing we are not merely seeking to see form. Rather, wilderness seasons invite us to see *beyond* what is visible or obvious. The function—or purpose—of eyes that see is to help us gain enhanced perspective.

Ra'ah

Ra'ah is a Hebrew verb meaning "to see," both literally and figuratively. Taking seeing to a deeper level, *ra'ah* implies gazing or looking at; discerning, inspecting, perceiving, considering; having vision.

In *Learning to Walk in the Dark*, professor and Episcopal priest Barbara Brown Taylor says: "Every major spiritual tradition in the world has something significant to say about the importance of paying attention."[1]

Author and firefighter Peter M. Leschak made this astute observation: "All of us are watchers—of television, of time clocks, of traffic on the freeway—but few are observers. Everyone is looking, not many are seeing."[2]

When we *ra'ah*, we see beyond what we are looking at. We pause to take a closer look. We examine. We pay attention.

Come Up Higher

I have been a runner for years; nothing invigorates me quite like the combination of fresh air and a challenging trail. During my extended wilderness season, I added in a rhythm of *walking* that became an essential practice. My framework for these calming times became "walk, look, and listen"—intentionally slowing down so I could develop seeing eyes. On days when I felt frustrated by the lack of clarity and tangible movement in my life, these walks gave me hope because I usually "saw" something through them.

On one such "walk, look, and listen" occasion, I was drawn to look up at the balcony-in-progress of a home under construction. As I took a closer look, I heard *Come up higher*—what I sensed to be an invitation to ask for enhanced perspective. From my limited vantage point down on the sidewalk, I could only see what I was in direct proximity to. But if I were to *come up higher*, my view would be expanded; I could see further.

Accepting this invitation became a rhythm for me throughout my wilderness years, especially in times of uncertainty or feeling stuck. I would choose to *come up higher* by asking God to show me my circumstances through the lens of divine perspective.

At a point of deep discouragement, I was standing outside thinking, *God, do you see me?* When I responded to the prompt to *look up*, what I saw took my breath away. Clouds shaped like a hand in the sky! It was as though I was staring at the palm of God's right hand. I was overwhelmed at the kindness displayed through this unique cloud arrangement—a tangible reminder that I was held and kept, cared for and seen.

In the area where I now live, hot air balloon sightings are common. Each time I get a glimpse of a brightly colored balloon floating above fields and homes, it is a reminder for me to *come up higher* and ask God for eyes that see beyond what is immediately visible.

Eyes that See at Thirty

In the Bible, the number thirty often represents a "right moment." Joseph was thirty when he was pulled from prison and positioned in the palace. David was thirty when he took the throne as king of Israel. Jesus was thirty when He received His rabbinic authority and began His earthly ministry.

I was thirty—nearly three years into the eleven-year wilderness season—when my eyes were opened through the avenue of significant spiritual dreams.

In the month that I began dreaming, I experienced a frightening impairment of vision. While I sat in an optometrist's waiting room with my physical eyes clouded over, my mind drifted back to the dream I'd had earlier that morning. In that "right moment," as I nervously waited to find out what was going on with my eyes, I vividly "saw" the meaning of my dream. It was a behind-the-scenes look at a painful situation that had happened months prior. The understanding offered through the dream brought comfort and closure.

Much to my relief, my physical vision returned to normal after a few days of intentional eye care, but my spiritual vision was never the same. I got a significant upgrade as my *seeing* eyes were opened.

For years after, I dreamed consistently, and had eyes to see what the dreams meant. I believe my enhanced vision came as a direct result of taking a closer look. Had I simply dismissed the dreams and gone on about my day, without pausing to record them and pay attention to what they might mean, I would have missed much insight that came through this unique avenue.

Moses On the Far Side of the Wilderness

As we look more closely at this posture of developing eyes that see, let's transition back to Moses, whose life can be viewed in three forty-year increments:

> forty years of luxury in Pharaoh's Egyptian palace
> forty years of obscurity in the wilderness, shepherding sheep
> forty years of leadership in the wilderness, shepherding a nation

In his address to the Sanhedrin in Acts 7, Stephen describes Moses as having been trained in all the wisdom of the Egyptians, powerful in both speech and action. Then he tells about the incident that sent forty-year-old Moses fleeing to Midian. In avenging his Hebrew brother by killing the Egyptian who was mistreating him, Stephen says, "Moses thought that his own people would realize that God was using him to rescue them, but they did not" (v. 25).

Forty years later, Moses was out tending his father-in-law Jethro's sheep. Leading the flock to the far side of the wilderness, Moses came to Horeb, the mountain of God. Exodus 3:2-3 tells us what happened next: "There the angel of the Lord appeared to him in flames of fire from within a bush. Moses saw that though the bush was on fire it did not burn up. So Moses thought, 'I will go over and see this strange sight—why the bush doesn't burn up.'"

Upon seeing that Moses had gone over to look, God called out to him from within the bush. This is one of only seven instances in Scripture when a person was addressed by name twice. Each time, something about that person's circumstances was primed for significant change.

Location, Location, Location

Perhaps you've heard it said that the number one rule of real estate is "location, location, location."

It is similar in Hebrew culture. Where an event occurs is never happenstance; location is purposeful and part of the greater narrative. Remember, Jewish readers approach Scripture asking, "What happened *here* before? What happened *like this* before?"

As we look at Moses in Exodus 3, two locations are teeming with importance:

1. The wilderness
2. Horeb, the mountain of God

Most of the time, when the mountain of God is referenced in the Bible, it is called Sinai. Yet in this case, the biblical author calls it by another name: *Horeb*, meaning "wasteland" or "desert."[3]

Humbled and forty years removed from the luxuries of Pharaoh's palace, eighty-year-old Moses encountered God *in the wilderness*, at the mountain of God known as Horeb, the *desert wasteland*. The double use of wilderness language is not happenstance. As we will soon discover, this narrative captures the potential wealth found in wilderness experiences. It reminds us that God finds us in the desert and will use even a barren landscape as the backdrop for powerful, life-altering encounter.

Names in the Middle East

As we continue journeying with Moses, it's important to gain some further cultural awareness.

Hebrew names tell you what the story should be about. If you know the meaning of a person's name, you have insight regarding the theme of their life.

For people in the ancient Near East, naming a child was highly significant. While modern-day parents may be prone to name their children in response to cultural trends or personal preference, often determining a name well before the child is born, Hebrew parents would choose a name based on what was happening around the time of the child's birth. In unique instances, God disclosed to the parents what they were to name a child before birth, indicating a distinct role that child was to embody.[4]

In modern Jewish culture, parents still wait eight days to name their children, giving them an opportunity to experience the baby's personality so they can then name them accordingly.

When reading the Bible, names provide clues to the story. For example,

Eve means "life"—her name was her destiny as she became the mother of the living.

Abraham means "father of many"—his name came to pass, as he was the patriarch who fathered many nations.

In antiquity, changing a person's name was one way a conquering ruler demonstrated their authority. For example, when Nebuchadnezzar besieged Jerusalem, Daniel and three of his Hebrew friends were taken captive and given Babylonian names, each of which included an allusion to pagan deities. This name change was an attempt to integrate them into Babylonian culture.[5]

So, what were these young men's new names? Daniel 1:7 tells us.

Daniel was renamed Belteshazzar; his Hebrew name means "God is my judge."

Hananiah, which implies "God has favored," was renamed Shadrach.

Mishael was renamed Meshach; his Hebrew name asks, "Who is what God is?"

Azariah, which means "Jehovah has helped," was renamed Abednego.

Even though these Hebrew men were taught foreign customs and given Babylonian names, God was with them and protected them: Hananiah, Mishael, and Azariah from the flames of the fiery furnace; and Daniel from the mouths of the lions. This divine safeguarding reflected the meanings of their original Hebrew names.

In other places in the Bible, parents named their children according to what was happening in the *parents'* lives when their child was born. For instance, Moses named his first son Gershom—meaning "a foreigner there"—because he had become a foreigner in the land of Midian.

Moses and Water

It was Pharaoh's daughter who adopted Moses and gave him his Egyptian name, which is *Moshe* (meaning "drawn out") in Hebrew.

Philo of Alexandria, a Hellenistic Jewish philosopher, claimed Moses' name was an allusion to the Egyptian word for water.[6] This is intriguing when we see how much of a recurring theme water was in Moses' life.

— He was drawn up out of the water after his Hebrew mother placed him in the Nile, to hide him from the genocidal Pharaoh. (Ex. 2:10)
— He protected Reuel's daughters from the shepherds at the well in Midian and drew water for their flocks. (Ex. 2:15–19)

— He struck the water of the Nile with his staff, and all the water was changed into blood. (Ex. 7:20)
— He led the Israelites through the salty waters of the Red Sea. (Ex. 14:13–16)
— He threw wood in the bitter water of Marah, and it became fit to drink. (Ex. 15:25)
— He struck the rock at Rephidim, and water came out for the people to drink. (Ex. 17:1–6)
— He was instructed by God to *speak* to the rock at Meribah when, once again, there was no water for the people. He disobeyed, striking the rock instead. (Num. 20:2–13)

A fascinating connection between Horeb and Moses is offered in the *NIV First-Century Study Bible*: "It must be noted that *Horeb* means 'dryness.' The water-drawing Moses, the future provider of water for the wandering people of God, met God on a mountain of barren dryness."[7]

We are just beginning to see the significance of names and locations throughout the biblical narrative.

Learning to Shepherd

As we will explore later, Moses' forty years shepherding *sheep* in the wilderness were preparing him for forty years of shepherding a *nation* through the wilderness.

Though Moses was a Hebrew by birth, being raised in Pharaoh's palace, immersed in Egyptian speech, dress, education, and customs made him irrelevant and out of touch with his people.

What transpired after Moses fled from Pharaoh demonstrates his Egyptian persona. As Moses was sitting by a well, the priest of Midian's seven daughters came to draw water for their father's flock. Other shepherds came along and chased the girls away. Moses jumped in and helped the girls, even taking time to water their flock. Upon returning to their father and telling him what had happened, the girls referred to the man who had rescued them as "an Egyptian." They did not recognize Moses as being a Hebrew.

Moses' middle forty years were his bridge back to the Hebrews. After being commissioned by God to deliver the Israelites, Moses returned to his people and they were ready to receive him (see Ex. 4:29-31).

From an external vantage point, Moses' forty years in the wilderness would have been a significant demotion. Egyptians looked down upon shepherds and Moses would have been acutely aware of this. To make circumstances even more personally humbling, the sheep Moses was shepherding were not even his; they were his father-in-law's.

In *The Gifts of the Jews*, Thomas Cahill describes Moses' time of refuge in Midian and his encounter with God at Horeb. "This strange land is about to yield up to this stranger the strangest experience ever known," says Cahill. "The text signals to us that something extraordinary is about to happen by calling this place [Horeb] 'the mountain of God,' but there is no reason to suspect that Moshe is anticipating anything more than another energy-sapping day with the flock."[8]

Moses began this day as he had so many others, in the desert shepherding sheep. But he would end it having been appointed to shepherd a nation.

The Bush That Was Not Burning Up

On the far side of the wilderness, at the mountain of God known as Horeb, the angel of the Lord appeared to Moses from the midst of a bush on fire but not consumed. Rather than noticing it and continuing on with the sheep, Moses stopped to take a closer look. Moses' pause compelled the living God to call to him from the bush.

When viewing this passage through a Western lens, the focus is often on the "burning bush" because that seems to be the unusual element. However, a bush on fire in the wilderness was not uncommon due to the high temperatures and dry heat. Moses had likely seen burning bushes before. The anomaly was that *this bush was not burning up*!

Rabbi Moshe David Cassuto says: "Although the bush (i.e. blackberry, Rubus Discolor) is commonly found in steppe country, and it is no unusual phenomenon for a bush dried by the summer's heat to catch fire, yet the bush that Moses saw was not consumed in the flame."[9]

Looking through a Western lens, we might ask, *How did this happen?* Through a Middle Eastern lens, our question shifts to: *Why would God manifest Himself through a bush in the wilderness?*

A citation from *midrash* (commentary) of the book of Exodus offers rabbinic perspective that the thorn bush symbolized Israel's slavery in Egypt: "Why did the Holy One, blessed be He, appear from the highest heavens and speak with Moses from within the bush? Because just as this bush was the thorniest of all the trees in the world . . . likewise was the slavery of Israel in Egypt the most oppressive slavery in the world."[10]

The *Babylonian Talmud* indicates that the bush was the lowliest of the thorn briars of the desert: "Bush, bush, it's not because you're higher than all other shrubs that the Holy One, blessed be He, brought his presence upon you, but because you're lower than all other trees he brought his Presence to rest on you."[11]

The Lord did not appear to Moses in a majestic tree, like a towering Lebanon cedar. Rather, He came in a much smaller thorn bush, in the wilderness at the wasteland known as Horeb.

Location matters.

Even when the location is a bush.

A Closer Look

Exodus 3 describes the moments that forever altered Moses' life—and the destiny of the Israelite nation—as he responded to the bush aflame yet not burning up. Notice how often the Hebrew word *ra'ah* is used:

> As Moses looked [*ra'ah*], he saw [*ra'ah*] that the bush was on fire but was not consumed. So Moses thought: I must go over and look at [*ra'ah*] this remarkable sight. Why isn't the bush burning up?
>
> When the Lord saw [*ra'ah*] that he had gone over to look [*ra'ah*], God called out to him from the bush, "Moses, Moses!" (vv. 2–4 HCSB)

In the midst of the mundane, as Moses happened upon a most unusual sight, he paused to take a closer look; he chose to *ra'ah*, to gaze at the bush.

In her *New York Times* bestseller, *An Altar in the World*, Barbara Brown Taylor identifies the inclination to turn aside as being what made this prince-turned-fugitive-turned-shepherd Moses. Deciding everything else he had going on could wait, Taylor says Moses "parked the sheep and left the narrow path in order to take a closer look at a marvelous sight. When he did, the storyteller says, God noticed. God dismissed the angel and took over the bush."[12]

For a shepherd to move toward the bush and away from his sheep would have been irresponsible; Moses was essentially putting the family's livelihood at risk. But by paying attention and inspecting the bush to determine why it wasn't burning up, he captured God's attention. In response, God spoke from the bush and introduced himself to Moses.

The caring heart of God is evident as He tells Moses that He has seen the misery of the Israelites in Egypt and has heard their cries. Concerned over the suffering they were experiencing, God says He is coming down to rescue them and take them to a land flowing with milk and honey. He then speaks words that no doubt caused tremors of terror and excitement in Moses: "'So now, go. I am sending you to Pharaoh to bring my people the Israelites out of Egypt'" (Ex. 3:10).

On the far side of the wilderness, after he paused to take a closer look at a fiery bush not devoured by the flames, Moses received his call to deliver the children of Israel from bondage in Egypt. This Moses was the same man they had rejected before.

Forty years shepherding sheep in obscurity, during which Moses developed eyes that perceived the needs and tendencies of the sheep he was responsible for, culminated in the stewardship of a moment.

Seeing eyes shifted the course of Moses' life.

Hagar's Plight

Now we revisit Hagar, our wilderness woman.

If you recall, Hagar's mistress, Sarai, was unable to conceive, so she gave Hagar to her husband, Abram, in hopes of having a family through her. Upon getting pregnant, Hagar began to treat her mistress with disdain. Sarai reacted by being abusive to Hagar, which sent Hagar fleeing into the wilderness. The angel of God found Hagar by a spring and asked what she was doing there. Hagar told the truth, and the angel instructed her to return to Sarai.

Before we continue, let's gain some cultural understanding as to what was happening within Abram's household.

Sarai's inability to have children was an unenviable stigma in an honor/shame culture, as barrenness evidenced the gods' displeasure towards a woman. The belief that deity opened and closed the womb is consistently communicated by the biblical authors, helping us grasp how culturally prevalent it was.

For example, Isaac prayed on behalf of childless Rebekah; God answered by enabling her to become pregnant. God allowed Jacob's unloved wife, Leah, to have numerous sons, while Rachel, his preferred wife, was barren for years. The Lord closed Hannah's womb for a season as well.

In her book *Daily Life in Biblical Times*, Liora Ravid describes the forlorn state of barren women, who lived day after day not knowing what sin they had committed to receive this punishment. "The God Who judged them with absolute justice had decreed they would be barren," writes Ravid. "For reasons they could not fathom, they had to bow their heads and stiffen their shoulders while arrows of scorn pierced their hearts."[13]

On top of the personal shame experienced, infertility could contribute to a fragile marriage environment. The primary cause for divorce, barrenness was viewed as the result of some deficiency in the woman.

Ravid offers further cultural perspective when she says, "women who had difficulty becoming pregnant occupied the lowest rung on the social ladder. A barren woman was a disgrace to herself and to her husband. His other wives exploited her weakness, mocking her and bolsting [sic] their own superior status."[14]

This understanding helps us better empathize with Sarai, who was living month after month, year after year, with the reality that she had not produced a son to continue Abram's family line. Adding to the pressure was the covenant promise that Abram's offspring would be as numerous as the sand on the seashore (see Gen. 12:2; 15:5)—though God did not specify that the covenant son would come through *Sarah* until Genesis 17. Abram's prompt consent when Sarai suggested he sleep with Hagar was a culturally acceptable way of handling infertility.

Looking through this lens also offers us a glimpse into the position Hagar was thrust into. Genesis 12:16 mentions "male and female servants" given to Abram by Pharaoh when the childless couple went to Egypt to avoid famine in the Negev; this is likely when they acquired Hagar. And it is noted at least *nine* times in Genesis 16 that Hagar was Sarai's servant, not Abram's. The biblical author is communicating that *Sarai* held the key to Hagar's future.

Sarai opted to give Hagar to Abram as another wife in hopes that she could "build a family through her" (Gen. 16:2). Dr. Sharon Pace, Professor of Hebrew Scriptures at Marquette University, says: "The phrase 'build up' does in fact refer to having a child, but it more importantly refers to establishing a people"[15]—similar to how "Rachel and Leah . . . together built up the family of Israel" (Ruth 4:11).

Ancient marriage contracts—including one from the town of Nuzi hundreds of years after the Patriarchal period—indicate that the potential of barrenness was taken into consideration. At times, a specific course of action was pre-determined, in case it became necessary to implement. This understanding makes it conceivable that Sarai, in giving Hagar to Abram, was simply putting the terms of their marriage contract into action. She was executing a viable solution.[16]

After being given to Abram, Hagar conceived. From a cultural perspective, it could appear as though the gods were more pleased with the Egyptian maidservant than with Sarai. We can appreciate how Hagar may have felt: that she was finally more than just a foreign servant and that she had a significant advantage over Sarai. If the gods showed favor to Hagar by allowing her to have a *son*, her status in the household would be strengthened even more.

Now we have a better grasp of the tensions within the family, and why

Sarai mistreated Hagar to the point that Hagar, pregnant and desperate, fled into the wilderness.

The God Who Sees

As Genesis 16 continues, the angel promises to give Hagar more descendants than she can count and tells her that she is pregnant with a son. Hagar is to name the boy Ishmael, meaning "God hears," because God has heard Hagar's cry of distress.

Hagar can mean "to flee" or "flight" and sounds like the Hebrew word *ger*, meaning "stranger" or "foreigner." Hagar was indeed a foreigner living in a Hebrew household. And she was on the run. This Egyptian maidservant had broken the law by fleeing from her mistress. Yet God found her in the wilderness... indicating that *He was looking for her*.

We perceive Hagar's essence as she confidently addressed the Lord: "You are the God who sees me"—*El Roi*.

The magnificence of this moment increases when we consider where Hagar had come from. Egypt was a polytheistic culture whose gods and goddesses who were *distant* and demanding. On the run, headed back towards Egypt by way of the road to Shur, Hagar encountered the Hebrew God who found her and *came close*.

Hagar, whose culture, class, and gender had kept her unseen, was finally seen. Being seen emboldened her to name God as she had experienced Him: *The God who sees me*.

By a well in the wilderness, the Hebrew God allowed a runaway Egyptian maid to be the first person Scripture records as naming Him. This audacious demonstration of impartiality would be mirrored thousands of years later when Jewish Jesus, God incarnate, also shattered cultural boundaries during His interaction with another woman at another well: the *Samaritan* woman at *Jacob's* well.

After Hagar named God, "that well was named Beer-lahai-roi (which means 'well of the Living One who sees me')" (Gen. 16:14 NLT).

From that time forward, every person who stopped to rest at this life-giving source of water in the wilderness was primed to receive, not just a refreshing drink, but assurance that *they too* were seen by the living God, as indicated by the well's name: *Beer-lahai-roi*.

The impact of Hagar's legacy is vast . . . like the Samaritan woman's after Jesus restored her honor.

El Roi, the *God who sees*, doesn't favor a certain gender, class, or ethnicity.

He saw Hagar in the wilderness.

He sees *us* in our wilderness.

Stringing the Pearls

Rabbinic teaching utilizes a concept called "stringing the pearls" that we too will incorporate as we journey together. It comes from the Hebrew word *charaz*, which describes putting together (stringing) various related passages of Scripture (pearls) to communicate an important lesson.

Think of it like this . . . while one pearl is beautiful, what's even more lovely are multiple pearls strung together in a necklace.

Rabbis and sages string together the pearls of Scripture to help their students better grasp the overarching meaning of the larger Story.

So let's string the pearls from Moses and Hagar.

Hundreds of years before God told Moses that He had been watching over the Hebrew people and had seen their oppression in Egypt, the *God who sees* saw an Egyptian maidservant being mistreated in a Hebrew household.

Prior to leading Moses and the Hebrews out of Egypt and through the wilderness, restoring their dignity after four centuries of slavery, the *God who sees* found an Egyptian slave woman in the wilderness and restored her honor.

Because we are made in the image of the *God who sees*, we can ask Him to give us eyes that see.

We don't have to wander aimlessly.

In our wilderness seasons, when we're feeling lonely, abandoned, lost, or hopeless, developing eyes that see can become our lifeline. We have an ongoing invitation to *ra'ah*. To pay attention. To take a closer look. To investigate.

DEVELOP EYES THAT SEE

In the words of philosopher and psychologist William James: "When we reach the end of our days, our life experience will equal what we paid attention to, whether by choice or default."

As we choose to see . . . to gaze at . . . to inspect, we are seen by *El Roi*, who meets us in our barren places.

Questions to Consider and *Yeshiva*

1. In what current circumstance do you need to *come up higher*? How might your perspective be enhanced if you do so?

2. Are you in the habit of stopping to look? If so, do you then take a closer look? If not, what hinders you?

3. Who or what is your gaze fixed on?

4. How does the lens you're looking through need to be adjusted?

5. What have you been staring at but not seeing?

6. In what ways have you experienced the *God who sees* seeing you?

5

CULTIVATE EARS THAT HEAR

> Only in the emptiness of the wilderness is the eye subordinate to the ear. Only in the silence of the desert can the sound beneath sound be heard.
> —Rabbi Jonathan Sacks

As we explore the third posture, *cultivate ears that hear*, we encounter another fundamental cultural difference between the West and Middle East.

You may remember that Western culture has been greatly influenced by Alexander the Great and the Hellenistic (Greek) mindset he perpetuated. On a foundational level, Hellenism is a *seeing* culture. For the ancient Greeks, truth was what they could perceive with their eyes. Hebraism, on the other hand, is a *hearing* culture. For the ancient Jews, truth was discovered through their ears.

Shema

If one word could sum up the difference between Western and Middle Eastern cultures, it would be *shema*.

In his work *Deuteronomy: Renewal of the Sinai Covenant*, Rabbi Jonathan Sacks provides a fascinating framework for discovering what is unique about a culture. "Search for words in its lexicon that are untranslatable into other languages," he says. "The Greek word *megalopsuchos*—literally, the 'great-souled' person, one blessed with wealth, status, and effortless superiority—has no equivalent in either Judaism or Christianity, two cultures that valued, as Greece did not, humility." Rabbi Sacks goes on to explain that "*shema* is untranslatable—understandably so since it belongs to biblical Hebrew, the world's supreme example of a culture of the ear.[1]

Shema is a verb meaning "to hear" or "to listen." It also implies acting, taking heed, and obeying. There is no biblical Hebrew word for "obey." Nearly every time we read the word "obey" in an English translation of the Old Testament, it comes from *shema*.

To *shema* is to hear the word of the Lord and live it out. To listen, understand, and respond as needed.

Some form of the root SH-M-A appears ninety-two times in Deuteronomy alone. For example: "Be silent, Israel, and listen [*ushema*, 'to pay focused attention']" (27:9).

Here is a variation used in Genesis 21:12; "Whatever Sarah says to you, do as she tells you [*shema bekolah*, 'to respond in action']."

In Exodus 18:24, Moses demonstrates the heart of *shema* by taking action: "Moses listened [*shema*] to his father-in-law and did everything he said."

When God came to Solomon in a dream and told him to ask for whatever he wanted, Solomon requested a "discerning" heart (see 1 Kings 3:9). In the Hebrew, it is *shema*. Solomon asked for a listening heart; not surprising considering his Jewish roots.

A *hearing* culture starkly contrasts today's secular culture, which is dominated by all things visual—from smartphones, computers, and tablets, to television and movies. A *seeing* culture is consumed by images and icons . . . that which can be perceived with the eyes.

To further substantiate the Middle Eastern *hearing* culture, we'll revisit a word used previously: *adhan*. Arabic for the Islamic call to prayer, the root of *adhan* is *adhina*, meaning "to listen, hear, or be informed about." Another derivative of this is *udhun*, which means "ear." Islam has a five-times-per-day rhythm built around hearing, a practice that compels them to pause, listen, and respond.

Western cultures have much to gain by learning from Middle Eastern *hearing* practices and values.

As we lean into this third posture, with *shema* as our focus, we are invited to consider these questions:

— Are we positioned to hear and respond?
— What hinders us from cultivating ears that hear?

Elijah's Journey

We first encountered Elijah the prophet in chapter three. As you recall, he was the one who staged a showdown between his God—the one true God—and the prophets of Baal and Asherah. Elijah's God won, after which he killed all the prophets of Baal with the sword.

On the heels of this enormous victory, Elijah was threatened by the wicked queen Jezebel, who had been killing off the Lord's prophets. Fearful for his life, Elijah fled to the wilderness. Then, 1 Kings 19 says,

> he came to a broom bush, sat down under it and prayed that he might die. "I have had enough, LORD," he said. "Take my life." Then he lay down under the bush and fell asleep.
>
> All at once an angel touched him and said, "Get up and eat." He looked around and there by his head was some bread baked over hot coals, and a jar of water. He ate and drank and then lay down again. (vv. 4–6)

In the next chapter, we'll dive deeper into Elijah's emotional state. Our focus now is his journey: *where* he was headed, *why* he was moving in that direction, and *what happened* when he got there.

Active in the Wilderness

In our first posture, *engage the process*, we discovered that each of us is invited to choose our *halakha,* or way of walking and living wilderness seasons. This includes determining whether we will be active participants or passive spectators.

As we consider Elijah's journey, it is evident that even in an emotionally low time, he chose to be active in the wilderness. When the angel of the

Lord returned, touching Elijah and again telling him to get up and eat, Elijah did as he had been instructed. Instead of staying under the broom bush, which was likely the only shade he encountered for several miles, Elijah left the measure of safety and comfort it provided. He made the forty-day trek to Horeb, the mountain of God, where he spent the night in a cave.

Throughout his prophetic, miracle-working ministry, Elijah had consistently experienced the power of God moving in *public* ways that were seen by others. Choosing to walk the path before him and be active in the wilderness positioned Elijah for a powerful *personal* encounter with the living God.

Location, Location, Location

When we think back to Moses on the far side of the wilderness, we recall that he encountered God at Horeb, in the bush that was not burning up.

If Elijah's flight to the wilderness is viewed through a Western lens, there can be a tendency to focus on his seeming lack of faith on the heels of his triumphant showdown with the false prophets. But when observed through a Middle Eastern lens, we recognize the significance of *where* Elijah ran—to the wilderness, headed toward Mount Horeb. If his goal were simply to escape Jezebel and her death threats, he could have fled countless other directions.

As a prophet, Elijah would have known Torah (the first five books of the Hebrew Bible) and been familiar with Moses' divine encounter at Horeb.

Pre–Mount Horeb, in Exodus 2, Moses was running from Pharaoh to the safety of Midian, located in the northwestern region of the Arabian desert. And while Elijah was indeed running from the wicked Jezebel, he was more importantly *running to* God at the *wasteland* in the wilderness. Even in his lowest moment, the direction Elijah chose indicates he may have been thinking something like, *If I can just make it to Horeb . . .*

When we take a closer look at the angel's words to Elijah, we see that they are assumptive—"Get up and eat, for the journey is too much for you" (1 Kgs 19:7)—as though the angel already knew where Elijah was headed and that he wasn't going to die under the bush in the wilderness.

When Elijah heard and responded, he was supernaturally empowered to walk the path before him.

Elijah's *halakha*—his way of walking and living—is worth emulating. He was emotionally low yet willfully moving in the direction of a place known for life-altering encounter with the living God.

Davar Bamidbar

In Hebrew, *davar* means "word" and *bamidbar* means "in the wilderness."

The approach toward Scripture in the West tends to be one of digging to pull out. But for a Middle Eastern Hebrew, the posture is one of receiving the word of the Lord that comes to or finds them, often *in* the wilderness—a *davar bamidbar*.

We see this as we journey forward with Elijah. Safely tucked away in the cave at Mount Horeb, this public prophet received a personal word from God, who spoke to him multiple times.

Elijah didn't have to go get the word of the Lord. Rather, he went to the place of previous encounter and positioned himself to receive the word that *found* him there.

A Still Small Voice

At Horeb, the living God didn't come in the mighty wind that tore the mountains apart and shattered the rocks. Nor did He come in the subsequent earthquake or fire.

God came in what has been translated as a "gentle and quiet whisper" (MSG); a "still small voice" (KJV); the "sound of a gentle blowing" (NASB).

In antiquity, powerful natural elements such as wind, earthquake, and fire were believed to be manifestations of the divine. The *Cultural Backgrounds Study Bible* explains: "The 'gentle whisper' is unusual and without parallel. In a theophany, the voice of the god usually thunders, but in all the destructive emanations there had been no message from Yahweh."[2]

Emphasizing how closely attuned Elijah's ears were, Rabbi Sacks says: "You can watch a storm, a fire, an earthquake, but you cannot see a still, small voice." Remember, the Hebrews are a *hearing* people, a culture of the ear. Rabbi Sacks continues: "Indeed the Hebrew is more pointed still: the words *kol demama daka* actually mean 'the sound of a thin silence,' which I define as *a voice you can hear only if you are listening.*"[3]

In other ancient religions, the gods were personified through nature: sun and stars, sky and seas, rain and storms. But the Hebrew God was and is the unseen *creator of* the natural elements worshipped as gods. Historian Heinrich Graetz says, "The pagan beholds his god; the Jew hears Him, that is, apprehends His will."[4]

Sometimes it takes a distraction-free desert to quiet our hearts and position us to hear the living God. We can *shema* the *davar* in the stillness of the *midbar*. We can hear the word in the silence of the wilderness.

Stringing the Pearls

When *El Roi*, the God who sees, saw Moses paying attention by pausing to look at the bush that wasn't burning up, He spoke.

When *El Roi* saw Elijah *shema* by responding to the gentle whisper and readying himself at the mouth of the cave, He spoke.

Both mighty men had life-changing encounters in the wilderness, at the *dry, desert wasteland* known as Horeb—the mountain of God.

The God who saw Moses and Elijah is watching our response as well. As we move toward Him, He moves towards us. We don't have to strive or strain; rather, we posture ourselves to receive.

Hagar and God Hears

Thus far, we've viewed Hagar's story through the lens of developing eyes that see; now we'll look from the vantage point of cultivating ears that hear.

Hagar knew she had been given to Abram for the sole purpose of producing descendants, since Sarai, up to that point, could not. God saw her in her story. Woman. Foreigner. Abused maidservant. Runaway. And carrying a child meant to solve her mistress's problem.

Having been mistreated by Sarai, Hagar was handled with great care by the Hebrew God in the wilderness. Not only did He find Hagar in her place of deep pain, but God also called her by name and did not condemn her for running away.

But that's not all. Hagar received a significant *davar bamidbar*. Her "word in the wilderness" was a promise that God would give her—a *female* in a male-oriented culture—more descendants than she could count. This type of action on behalf of a woman was unheard-of in that day and time!

God followed through on His promise. Thousands of years later, Hagar is recognized in Judaism, Christianity, and Islamic tradition, the latter of which refers to her as the "Grand Mother of Arabians."

God even provided specifics about the child she was carrying. She was going to have a son, and she was to name him *Ishmael*, meaning "God hears"—a constant reminder that the Hebrew God had heard her cry of distress; He paid attention to her misery.

Through His intentional interaction with Hagar, we see the living God modeling the heart of *shema*; He heard, listened, and responded. Because God heard her, Hagar felt seen—perhaps for the first time ever.

Life as a servant—being treated as *property* more than a person—was certainly its own type of wilderness. Yet it was also this difficult context that positioned Hagar to be given to a Hebrew family and eventually encounter God in the wilderness, unique space where she experienced His redemptive nature.

Hagar's *Chutzpah*

I like to envision Hagar returning to Abram and Sarai from the wilderness, having encountered *El Roi*, the God Who Sees, and carrying within her *Ishmael*, God Hears.

Was her face radiant? Was there a spring in her step? Was she more confident?

The angel had instructed Hagar to go back and submit to her mistress, yet her return may have been about far more than her responsibility as Sarai's servant. Hagar's essence and the child she carried communicated a message that Sarai and Abram desperately needed to be reminded of as they waited for the covenant to come to pass: *God Sees* and *God Hears*—even when it feels like the promise is never going to be fulfilled.

Hagar had a certain way about her that I like to call *Hagar's chutzpah* (pronounced *hoots-pa*). In *Walking in the Dust of Rabbi Jesus*, Lois

Tverberg describes *chutzpah* as "sheer audacity that borders on obnoxiousness."[5] Hagar clearly possessed unusual bravery and boldness. After all, what runaway Egyptian maidservant has the courage to speak with and then name the Hebrew God? No doubt her *chutzpah* intensified after this wilderness encounter.

She was no longer just an Egyptian servant. She had been seen and heard by the Hebrew God, and she returned carrying her own promise from Him.

Genesis 16 ends in a way that is easy to overlook, yet its significance runs deep. Verse 15 says: "So Hagar bore Abram a son, and Abram gave the name Ishmael to the son she had borne."

Nowhere does the text say God spoke the name Ishmael to Abram, such as He did in the very next chapter, when telling Abraham to call the son to be born to Sarah by the name Isaac (Gen. 17:19). Or as God would later communicate to Joseph in a dream to name his son Jesus (see Matt. 1:20–21) and Zechariah through an angelic encounter to name his son John (see Luke 1:13).

So how did Abram know to name his son Ishmael?

While Scripture doesn't explicitly say it, we can consider the likelihood that Hagar, upon returning from the wilderness, told Abram about her encounter with the angel of the Lord—including what the son she carried within her womb was to be named. And this Hebrew patriarch chose to *shema*. He listened . . . to an Egyptian maidservant.

Chutzpah. Hagar had it.

Shmatikha

In Genesis 17, God changed Abram's name to Abraham, promising to make him the father of many nations. He also changed Sarai's name to Sarah, guaranteeing she would have a son and be the mother of nations.

It is within this context that we are exposed to another form of *shema*, demonstrating the depth of meaning beyond "to hear." It is *shmatikha*, which implies internalizing and taking to heart; considering what has been said as a weighty matter; bearing it in mind.

Abraham was, understandably, struggling to believe that he, at one hundred years old, and Sarah, at ninety, would have a biological child. He requested that God allow it to be Ishmael who lived under His blessing. In response, God reiterated that Sarah would have the covenant son, whom they would name Isaac.

Speaking to Abraham's innate paternal desire, God said: "'As for Ishmael, I have heard you [*shmatikha*]: I will surely bless him; I will make him fruitful and will greatly increase his numbers. He will be the father of twelve rulers, and I will make him into a great nation'" (Gen. 17:20).

God heard Abraham's request, considered it, and responded. By promising to make Ishmael into a great nation, God affirmed the promise previously made to Hagar—that her descendants would be too numerous to count.

Ishmael: God Hears

Had Hagar and Ishmael remained in Abraham's household, Ishmael would have had a right to share in the inheritance. This posed a threat to Isaac, the newborn son of the covenant promise. So, Sarah took decisive action to be sure her son wasn't at risk. Hagar was given her freedom—by being sent away, along with fourteen-year-old Ishmael—so that he would no longer be a legitimate heir.

Once more, we meet Hagar in the wilderness, rejected and afraid. And as if that weren't enough, now Hagar and Ishmael had run out of water, a sure sign that death was imminent. In contrast to her previous wilderness encounter where *seeing* was the focal point of her naming God, Hagar now averts her eyes as watching her son die of thirst was too much.

She was crying.

He was crying.

And God heard.

Once again, the angel of God found Hagar, this time encouraging her not to fear because the living God had heard Ishmael's cries. The promise of Ishmael becoming a great nation was repeated.

Genesis 21 tells us that God opened Hagar's eyes, showing her a well of water. She went to it and filled her water container, then gave Ishmael a drink.

God hears and responds.

The *God who sees* opens eyes.

In the barren wilderness, the lives of Hagar and Ishmael were spared by these realities.

Hear. Listen. Respond.

Just as we are made in the image of the *God Who Sees*, which gives us confidence to ask for eyes that see, so are we made in the image of the *God Who Hears*. The God who pursues and finds us in the wilderness, and lovingly listens to our cries of distress.

His heart is to *shema*—to hear and respond, so much so that He placed within the womb of a rejected Egyptian maidservant a son who would become the father, not only of twelve princes, but of a great nation. Ishmael's name would ever remind Hagar that the Hebrew God hadn't just seen her but had *heard* her as well.

Opportunities to *shema* are ever before us. To hear. To listen. To respond. With assurance, we can ask God to help us *cultivate ears that hear*, so that those opportunities don't pass us by.

Jeremiah's Invitation to Ask

As we close out this posture, let's briefly look at the experience of another Hebrew prophet.

Jeremiah was often known as a "prophet of doom" and the "weeping prophet" because he frequently expressed his anguish of spirit (see Jeremiah 4:19; 9:1; 23:9).

In what we might consider a circumstantial "wilderness," the word of the Lord came to Jeremiah *while he was imprisoned*. Having been confined by Zedekiah king of Judah, Jeremiah was being held in the courtyard of the guard in the royal palace of Judah.

Jeremiah didn't have to go seeking out the word of the Lord. Just as God found Moses and Elijah at Horeb, and Hagar by a spring in the wilderness, so He also found Jeremiah in prison. This is what God said: "'Ask me and I will tell you remarkable secrets you do not know about things to come'" (Jer. 33:3 NLT).

In a barren situation, God told Jeremiah to call out to Him. And the God who hears promised, "I will answer you."

In my extended wilderness season, this passage was a bright ray of hope, a desert deposit that multiplied over time. The reality that God had great and mysterious things to share with me, too, was incredibly promising, especially in a prolonged and quiet wilderness season.

I took God at His Word and began asking, and as promised, He heard me and responded.

"To receive the Word of God," says Rabbi Sacks, "we must make ourselves open, the way a desert is. We have to engage in active listening . . . We need an open mind and a receptive heart."[6] Each of us would be wise to *shema* his counsel.

Questions to Consider and *Yeshiva*

1. Are you positioned to hear? If not, why not? If so, what are you hearing?

2. What *davar bamidbar* ("word in the wilderness") have you received from the Lord?

3. How is your hearing impaired or enhanced through wilderness seasons?

4. In what ways have you been hearing, yet not responding?

5. If cultivating ears that hear is difficult for you, what are you being hindered by?

6

EXPRESS AUTHENTIC EMOTIONS

> Emotions are like messengers from the front line
> of the battle zone. Our tendency is to kill the messenger.
> But if we listen carefully, we will learn how
> to fight the war successfully.
> —Dan Allender & Tremper Longman III

Our next posture involves the third of our senses that can be enhanced in wilderness seasons. We have learned the importance of developing eyes that see and cultivating ears that hear; now we discover the value in *expressing authentic emotions*.

Lev

The Hebrew word serving as the foundation for this posture is *lev*, meaning "heart." In the ancient Near East, the heart was not only the seat of the emotions, but it also encompassed the mind, will, and thoughts. The heart was the center of the inner life. This perspective helps us better grasp the admonition in Proverbs 4 to diligently guard or watch over our hearts. It also provides insight as to why "heart" occurs over one thousand times in Scripture.

We see *lev* used in Psalm 119 as the author describes the importance of pursuing God and His word:

I seek you with all my heart [*lev*]; do not let me stray from your commands. I have hidden your word in my heart [*lev*] that I might not sin against you. (vv. 10-11)

If the heart is our source of life, it would stand to reason that we should be paying attention to its messages—*especially* during wilderness seasons. But sometimes we need permission to do so and a framework for how, particularly if faulty beliefs about our emotions, or unhealthy emotional outbursts, have jaded our understanding of the importance of giving voice to deep heart matters.

Throughout this chapter, as we examine the range of emotions expressed in the wilderness by Elijah, Moses, Hagar, and David, be mindful of how God responded in each scenario. But first, let's observe what Scripture says about the hearts of two Israeli kings.

Desert Difficulty versus Palace Privilege

David, who would become the second king of Israel, grew up in Bethlehem, shepherding his father's sheep in the wilderness (see 1 Sam. 16:11; 17:28). Years later, he fled to the wilderness as a place of refuge and safety when King Saul, and even his own son Absalom, sought to take his life. David experienced the harsh wilderness elements, along with the sanctuary and shelter offered by the desert caves and waterfall-rich oasis of En Gedi, where he penned multiple psalms.

In contrast, the Bible doesn't seem to indicate that Solomon, David's son and the third king of Israel, considered one of the wisest and wealthiest men to ever live, spent any time in the wilderness. Solomon was a product of palace privilege (as Moses too was shaped by forty years in Pharaoh's palace) and was eventually given the throne. He knew a life of relative ease; anything he desired was within his reach.

Consider the description of Solomon in 1 Kings 11:1-3, paying close attention to what is said about his posture towards foreign women:

> King Solomon, however, loved many foreign women besides Pharaoh's daughter . . . They were from nations about which the Lord

had told the Israelites, "You must not intermarry with them, because they will surely turn your hearts after their gods." Nevertheless, Solomon held fast to them in love. He had seven hundred wives of royal birth and three hundred concubines, and his wives led him astray.

In the ancient Near East, kings would acquire foreign wives to build and strengthen diplomatic alliances with other nations. What's so interesting about this passage is that multiple times it references Solomon's *love for* these women. They were not just a political power play for him; they had his heart.

1 Kings 11:4 goes on to say that as "Solomon grew old, his wives turned his heart after other gods, and his heart was not fully devoted to the Lord his God, as the heart of David his father had been."

Years earlier, before David had become king, the prophet Samuel described him as a man after God's own heart (see 1 Sam. 13:14). Long after Solomon had taken over the throne—as well as other kings after him, David's heart was said to have been "fully devoted to the Lord his God" (1 Kings 15:3).

The wilderness seems to have done its refining work in David. From his early days shepherding sheep, to fleeing for his life and relying on God for protection and provision. In the wilderness, he was invited to seek God with all his heart; to desire God as one longs for water in a parched desert land.

In the wilderness, David encountered God in ways Solomon's affluent circumstances could not afford him the opportunity to do. Scripture doesn't indicate that Solomon ever had to trust God for daily bread in the desert. He didn't have to deal with the unruly heat while simultaneously searching for drinkable water and seeking refuge from enemies. David fled to the wilderness while being pursued by those intent on killing him. In contrast, Solomon's ego was stroked by those seeking out his wisdom and admiring the grandeur in which he lived.

Where David was shaped by difficulty in the desert, Solomon never got to exercise those muscles. This deficit left him lacking and open, prone to fill voids with women and wealth, power and prestige.

Elijah's Exhaustion

We've looked at Elijah several times already; now we'll do so mindful of the authentic emotions he expressed.

Remember from previous chapters that after Elijah had bested the prophets of Baal—then killed them—Queen Jezebel, known murderer of the prophets of God, determined to kill him. Afraid and fleeing for his life, Elijah left his servant in Beersheba and continued into the wilderness.

While traveling through the wilderness alone isn't safe or recommended, we can empathize with Elijah's disposition. The freedom to fully express himself emotionally, as a prolific man of influence, would likely have been restrained had his servant or others made the journey with him.

I Kings 19:4 says: "He came to a broom bush, sat under it and prayed that he might die. 'I have had enough, LORD,' he said. 'Take my life.'" Elijah was depressed and overwhelmed; so much so that he asked God to kill him. Being afraid, on the run, tired, and isolated, were all factors contributing to Elijah's declining emotional state.

As Elijah slept under a bush, he was able to temporarily escape. This larger-than-life prophet becomes very human in these moments. Relatable. He was exhausted and wanted a reprieve from his circumstances . . . a break from the pressure to be "on" and to have to perform in front of countless numbers of people, including the king. He needed time alone, with only his own thoughts to consider, as opposed to speaking a word from God to a nation. And he desperately needed refuge from the wicked queen.

Even in such an emotionally low place, Elijah was active in the wilderness. When the angel woke him from his sleep, telling him to get up and eat, Elijah chose to *shema*. He heard the angel and responded. He got up and ate . . . and then he fell asleep again. We can almost feel the depth of Elijah's exhaustion.

Interestingly, for Elijah, being fed by an angel in the wilderness did not seem to be anything unusual. It was just another day in the life of this extraordinary prophet!

The angel came and touched Elijah again, saying, "'Get up and eat some more, or the journey ahead will be too much for you'" (1 Kings

19:7). Once more Elijah chose to *shema*. He heard and responded, and in so doing, as we learned previously, he received supernatural strength for the forty-day trek to Horeb.

While he was fearful and running *from* Jezebel, emotionally low and physically exhausted, Elijah was running *to* the living God at Horeb, the very mountain where Moses had encountered God as I AM.

Upon arriving, Elijah spent the night in a cave. The Lord spoke to him, inquiring as to what he was doing there. Elijah's response—that he was the *only* prophet of God left—reveals a significantly distorted perspective. What he states as truth was not accurate. God would soon let him know there were seven thousand other prophets who had not bowed to Baal.

When the Lord told Elijah to stand before Him on the mountain, Elijah chose to *shema* yet again. He heard and responded by moving to the front of the cave, positioning himself for encounter with the divine.

Again, God asked what Elijah was doing there, to which he answered as he had previously. Real or not real, Elijah felt like he was the only God-fearing prophet still alive, and he expressed this sentiment openly.

Instead of speaking directly to Elijah's honest but erroneous answer, God summoned him up and out of that low place, out of isolation and back into his calling. He gave Elijah a *visionary directive*, telling him where to go and what to do. There was an enormous transfer of power about to take place, and Elijah would be the prophetic catalyst.

But... there was a catch to the instructions God had given: Elijah was to go back *the way he had come*—in the very direction he had run from to escape Jezebel.

In her bestselling book, *Braving the Wilderness*, Brené Brown writes about showing up as one's true self, and the "wilderness" of uncertainty and criticism that often follows. Elijah knew this well. When he "showed up" by speaking from the fullness of his prophetic mantle, drought fell on the Northern Kingdom for three-and-a-half years. The drought culminated after Elijah called down fire from heaven, outdoing Jezebel's beloved prophets of Baal. These scenarios sparked outrage from those who refused to humble themselves before the Hebrew God whom Elijah represented.

Brown says: "Belonging so fully to yourself that you're willing to stand alone *is* a wilderness—an untamed, unpredictable place of solitude and searching. It is a place as dangerous as it is breathtaking, a place as sought after as it is feared."[1] Elijah had ample time for soul-searching during his forty-day solo trek to Horeb—liminal space between his encounters with the angel in the wilderness and God at the mountain. He then had a choice: stay hidden in the cave, or step back into who he was called to be, which would require returning, *alone*.

Remember, this is the same Elijah who twice expressed to God his concern at being "the only one left." A significant shift occurred as Elijah braved, not only the harsh elements of the external wilderness, but also the internal wilderness inviting him to reconnect with himself and courageously face his fears.

Think back to our first posture, *engage the process*. It was noted that some wilderness seasons are so intense that survival itself is the victory. Yet if our overall posture is to thrive in and through the wilderness, even in moments of survival, we will revert to thriving. We see this embodied in Elijah.

As a prophet whose role was to hear from God and relay that message publicly to the people, Elijah positioned himself privately to *shema*. In so doing, he received a *davar bamidbar*, his word in the wilderness. This word was a commissioning for Elijah to go anoint two new kings, as well as the prophet who would succeed him.

In other words, at Elijah's lowest point, God heard his authentic emotional expression and responded in a way that communicated, "I'm not finished with you. There's still work for you to do." God may as well have said, "Jezebel is *not* going to kill you—at least not yet!"

The reality of this this word from the living God flowing through Elijah's being as he went back the way he had come, likely lit him on fire.

A word in the wilderness changes us.

Elijah didn't just hear the visionary directive; he received it and acted on it. But first, he expressed his authentic emotions, including asking God to kill him.

In our wilderness seasons, when we convey our feelings openly and honestly to God, he hears and responds. He calls us up and out of dark places in a way that cuts through the emotional haze and brings clarity for the path ahead.

Moses' Frustration

Guiding any group of people through the wilderness for an extended period would have its challenges, so the reality of Moses directing a young nation coming out of slavery and oppression was an entirely different kind of leadership test.

There were moments when Moses was faith-filled and valiant, and others when he'd had enough, such as the scenario detailed in Numbers 11. A group described as "the rabble" traveling with the Israelites began to crave the comforts of Egypt. Their perspective was distorted as they recalled the food they had eaten there "at no cost," although the high cost they had been paying was their freedom.

Moses expressed his raw emotions through a lengthy rant, questioning why God had brought this trouble on him, and what he had done to deserve the burden of these people. Overwhelmed by their complaints, as well as the responsibility of finding meat for the masses, Moses was at a breaking point. He conceded that he couldn't continue to carry the Israelites alone.

In a moment of total frustration, Moses told God, "'If this is how you are going to treat me, please go ahead and kill me—if I have found favor in your eyes—and do not let me face my own ruin'" (Num. 11:15). Moses was so overwhelmed that he asked God to put him out of his misery.

Once again God modeled *shema*. He heard Moses' emotional expression and, as with Elijah, He didn't address Moses' emotions. Rather, He responded by offering a practical solution that would allow Moses to share the responsibility of leadership with seventy Israelites elders instead of shouldering the burden on his own.

Moses, like Elijah, chose to *shema*. He listened to God and responded by taking immediate action. By first giving voice to his heart he experienced the living God come to his aid.

Hagar's Hopelessness

By now we have become more familiar with Hagar. As we view her story through the lens of expressing authentic emotions, we will again see the Hebrew God moving on her behalf.

Remember that Hagar and her son Ishmael had been sent away by the couple who had once sheltered them. On their own in the wilderness, they had run out of water. Hopeless and unable to bear watching Ishmael die, Hagar separated herself from him; then she sat down and "broke into sobs" (Gen. 21:16 MSG).

God heard the fear-filled emotional expressions of Hagar and Ishmael. He answered their desperate cries by reiterating His promise of offspring for Ishmael, thus offering hope that they were going to live. Then He gave Hagar eyes to see the well of lifesaving water.

And this time, the angel addressed Hagar without adding "slave of Sarai" as in their previous encounter. The biblical author portrays the angel as acknowledging Hagar's plight: no longer bound to her former mistress yet untethered from a familial covering responsible for providing she and her son's basic needs.

David's Desire

In Psalm 63:1, David expresses different types of emotions to God than what we've encountered with Elijah, Moses, and Hagar. David doesn't voice fear or depression or anguish, but rather, deep longing and desire. He says: "Oh God, you are my God; I earnestly search for you. My soul thirsts for you; my whole body longs for you in this parched and weary land where there is no water" (NLT).

The Message (MSG) says it like this: "God—you're my God! I can't get enough of you! I've worked up such hunger and thirst for God, traveling across dry and weary deserts."

This wasn't just poetic language for David. He had experienced the reality of fleeing to the wilderness multiple times, relying on God for protection and provision. David knew firsthand what it was like to thirst deeply for water in the wilderness; he also understood experientially that God was the only one who could satisfy his soul-thirst.

Stringing the Pearls

As we string the pearls, we see some similarities.

All were in a wilderness: Elijah in the Desert of Sinai. Moses in the Desert of Paran. Hagar in the Desert of Beersheba. And David in the Judean wilderness.

All poured out their emotions to God: Elijah was exhausted. Moses was frustrated. Hagar felt hopeless. And David desired.

God responded to these biblical characters' emotional expressions by inviting them to actively participate with Him *through* the wilderness.

> Elijah went to anoint.
> Moses appointed seventy elders.
> Hagar drew water from the well.
> David worshipped.

In our wilderness seasons, God can handle the depth of *our* emotions too. When He becomes our primary go-to for emotional expression, we can safely release feelings, questions, and disappointments. And by going to God first, we lessen the likelihood of unhealthy emotional "venting"... which may include seeking out people who will rescue us from having to take personal responsibility and necessary action.

There is deep value in expressing our authentic emotions. In our wilderness seasons, God hears each cry of our heart, and He faithfully responds.

Questions to Consider and *Yeshiva*

1. How does Elijah's humanity—his emotional expression in the wilderness—encourage and/or challenge you?

2. When has the burden of responsibility been its own type of wilderness season for you? Did you allow your heart to "speak" by expressing your emotions to God?

3. How does Moses' earnest request for God to take his life free you to be more open and honest with God? Have you ever made a similar appeal? What might you have missed had God granted your request?

4. When has God heard your cry or frustration in a wilderness season and responded?

5. Describe a wilderness season when your hunger and thirst for God deepened. Why do you think that desire intensified?

6. How do you need to be more honest with yourself, God, and others regarding the emotions you are feeling?

7

PERCEIVE ENCOUNTERS WITH THE DIVINE

> If the concept of the Mishkan, the Tabernacle, is that God lives in the human heart whenever it opens itself unreservedly to heaven, then its physical location is irrelevant . . .
> If God is everywhere, He can be reached anywhere.
> —Rabbi Jonathan Sacks

The wilderness uniquely positions us to *perceive encounters with the divine*—our fifth posture—in ways that no other place or season can. As distractions lessen and dependency increases, as we are simultaneously emptied and filled, we are readied to receive and oftentimes more aware of the divine in our midst.

Mishkan

The Hebrew word anchoring us in this posture is *mishkan*, meaning "tabernacle." *Mishkan* suggests a desert dwelling or temporary tent. The Israelites were commanded to construct the tabernacle as a visual representation of God's presence among them. *Mishkan* is used repeatedly throughout Exodus 25–40 as God instructs the Israelites in the specific details of the tabernacle. For example, in Exodus 25:9 God said: "Make this tabernacle [*mishkan*] and all its furnishings exactly like the pattern I will show you."

The root of *mishkan* is shared with *Shekinah*, one of the most significant Hebrew words for God's *divine presence* or *nearness*. Another related

Hebrew word is *kavod*, which means "glory" and implies *weightiness* or *divine presence*, as used in Exodus 40:34, along with *mishkan*: "Then the cloud covered the tent of meeting and the glory [*kavod*] of the LORD filled the tabernacle [*mishkan*]."

The presence of the Lord *with and among* is what set the Israelites apart from other nations. Never before had a deity walked with its people. Yet the Lord told Moses that His presence would go with Moses and the people, and that He would give them rest.

The desire for this differentiation is felt in Moses' response:

"If your Presence does not go with us, do not send us up from here. How will anyone know that you are pleased with me and with your people unless you go with us? What else will distinguish me and your people from all the other people on the face of the earth?" (Ex. 33:15–16)

The Lord reiterated that, because He was pleased with Moses and knew him by name, He would do what Moses had asked.

Throughout this posture, we will see God traveling with and among the Israelites during their wilderness years, coming close in a way that was relatable to them. The *mishkan*, God's portable, temporary tent, mirrored the Israelites' portable, temporary desert tents—a tangible reminder that God always meets His people where they are, but He doesn't leave them there.

A life-size model, based on the specifications set by God in Exodus, is located at Timna Park in Israel's Negev desert or arabah region. The *mishkan* was not grandiose in size at 150 feet by 75 feet. But the glory of the Lord filled it anyway.

God traveling with and dwelling among. *Mishkan* invites us to greater awareness of how we are encountering the living God through our wilderness seasons.

Divine Proximity

The God of the Hebrews was doing something unheard-of in a day and time when gods were typically distant. While the Israelites were still enslaved to Pharaoh in Egypt, God spoke to Moses, inviting them to worship Him at Mount Sinai in the wilderness.

Commentary from the *Cultural Backgrounds Study Bible* offers this perspective: "That one particular mountain was referred to as God's mountain is intriguing. Ancient Near Eastern deities often had their dwelling place on a mountain. In the mythology of Ugarit in Syria, e.g., Baal had his palatial abode on Mount Zaphon (Jebel el-Aqra in Western Syria) about 25 miles north of Ugarit."[1]

The living God was meeting the Israelites in a way they would understand, while also showing Himself to be a different kind of deity. Instead of staying far away, the Hebrew God came close at Sinai, then left His mountain to travel with and dwell among them.

In an interview with Dr. Miroslav Volf, whom I introduced in chapter 3, Rabbi Jonathan Sacks expounds on this idea. He says: "What is at the heart of Judaism is the sense that God is somebody very close. This is not a philosopher's God; this a God who takes us by the hand and leads us through the sea and steers us through the wilderness." Rabbi Sacks explains that "the Hebrew word for divine presence, *Shekinah*, is, in secular language, the next-door neighbor—so this is God as the next-door neighbor.[2]

Divine Presence Distinguishes

After escaping from Egypt, the Israelites experienced divine presence as the Lord went ahead of them in ever-present pillars: a cloud to guide them by day, and fire that provided light and direction at night.

Once Pharaoh realized the labor force he had lost by letting the Israelites go, he and his charioteers chased after them, hemming them in at the Red Sea. What unfolded is a story of miraculous intervention that has been told and retold for thousands of years.

The angel of God that had been travelling in front of the Israelite army relocated behind them. The pillar of cloud did as well, providing a divine barrier between the Egyptians and Israelites. The cloud brought darkness to one side and light to the other all throughout the night, preventing them from going near each other.

Divine presence was *visible* to the Israelites through their wilderness years. God's presence is *available* to us today through our wilderness seasons. He went before the Israelites in a pillar of cloud by day and pillar of fire by night. He goes before us in ways seen and unseen, giving us courage and wisdom to navigate our wilderness path.

God met the Israelites at Sinai (see Exodus 19), then left His mountain to be *with and among* them as they journeyed through the wilderness (see Num. 10:11-12, 33-34). They lived in temporary tents, so God lived in a temporary tent: the *mishkan*, or tabernacle.

Today, He lives in our "temporary tents," dwelling within each of us who love Him. In the words of a well-respected rabbi, "Divine Presence lives . . . not in a physical place but in the human heart."[3]

It was divine presence, Shekinah, that set the Israelites apart from every other nation.

Remember, divine presence also distinguished Hagar, Moses, and Elijah. Hagar encountered the angel of the Lord by a spring in the wilderness. Moses encountered "I AM" in the bush that was not burning up at Horeb. Elijah encountered the angel of the Lord in the wilderness, and the Lord Himself at the mouth of a cave at Horeb.

God always meets us where we are, but He doesn't leave us there.

Divine Presence Offers Rest

The God of the Hebrews provided another unique gift connected to His presence. For 430 years, the nation of Israel had only known slavery and forced labor. Now a new *halakha*, or way of living, was being offered to them. In Exodus 33:14, God promises: "'My Presence will go with you, and I will give you rest.'"

God met the children of Israel in their post-captivity mindset. They were used to being told what to do by cruel, demanding taskmasters. In the wilderness, God's presence guided them, showing them when to move on and when to remain. They could rest *mentally* and *emotionally* as they learned to trust and look to Him for guidance. They could rest *physically* when the pillars of cloud and fire lingered in a location.

God was welcoming dependence on Him by positioning them to not have to think beyond the pillars of cloud and fire. His presence with and among them offered rest from striving and straining.

Divine presence offers us rest too.

Divine Pursuit

In our wilderness seasons, God pursues us . . . inviting us to experience and encounter Him.

When Hagar escaped into the wilderness, the Hebrew God "found her" (Gen. 16:7), implying He was looking for her.

During the Israelites' wilderness years, God "found them" (Deut. 32:20), suggesting He was searching and watching out for them.

The prophet Hosea later recorded the marriage language used in God's ongoing pursuit of the Israelites: "'Therefore I am now going to allure her; I will lead her into the wilderness and speak tenderly to her' . . . 'In that day,' declares the Lord, 'you will call me *my husband*. . . I will betroth you to me forever'" (2:14, 16, 19).

As introduced earlier, the Hebrews' went into the wilderness expecting to receive a *davar bamidbar*—a "word in the wilderness." This word came to them, just as it did for Hagar the Egyptian, Moses, Elijah—and John the Baptist, as described in Luke 3:2, when "the word of God came to John son of Zechariah in the wilderness."

They didn't have to *go get* the word of the Lord; rather, it found them as God pursued them in the wilderness.

Hagar's *Davar Bamidbar*

Returning momentarily to Hagar, we've seen that her gender, class, and ethnicity gave her no reason to anticipate divine pursuit.

But when the angel of the Lord found her in the wilderness, he spoke a word of *visionary hope*—that God was going to make a great nation from her son. This *davar* was repeated years later, when the angel again found she and Ishmael in the wilderness, thirsty and afraid, expecting to die.

Moses' *Davar Bamidbar*

On the far side of the wilderness, at the mountain of God known as Horeb, Moses received a *call to deliver*. This unexpected meeting summoned Moses into his role as liberator.

In my eleven-year wilderness season, which at times seemed endless, I often looked to Joseph's journey from pit to prison to palace (detailed in Genesis 37-50) for encouragement that God was indeed at work, even when I couldn't see evidence of it. Joseph endured a thirteen-year "wilderness" that included betrayal, false accusation, and imprisonment. As I contemplated Joseph's path, and the moment his trajectory dramatically changed, a phrase emerged within me that I often remind myself of:

It takes God a long time to act suddenly.

Moses was in the wilderness region of Midian shepherding sheep—as he'd done day after day, year after year—when He encountered God in the bush that was not burning up. His years of lavish living in Pharaoh's palace were likely a distant memory.

It took God a long time—*forty years*—to act suddenly in Moses' life. But that "suddenly" moment brought a *davar* that propelled Moses into his destiny.

Elijah's *Davar Bamidbar*

Elijah entered the wilderness weary, discouraged, and fleeing for his life, while at the same time running toward Horeb—the place of Moses' encounter with God.

Elijah's *davar bamidbar* was a *visionary directive*, a commissioning of sorts. New kings were to be anointed, and a new prophet would arise. So, what did Elijah do upon receiving his word? He left Horeb and found Elisha.

Elijah chose to walk the path before him—the path that could put him back on Jezebel's radar and in harm's way—but would ultimately place him in a chariot of fire, spiraling up to heaven in a whirlwind (see 2 Kings 2:11).

No doubt the transformation in and on Elijah was palpable from the time he went into the wilderness, depressed and exhausted, to the time he emerged, determined and assured.

A word from God can alter the course of our lives.

Roses from Heaven

Through my eleven-year wilderness season, I received *devarim* (words) that gave me hope and were anchors to return to. Repeatedly I experienced the living God pursuing me in my wilderness.

As a thirty-year-old, three different times when I was visiting my sister and her family, I received roses on the windshield of my car. These roses had an otherworldly aroma—rich, deep, and sweet. The roses always came in a snack-size bag, at a time when I felt desperate to hear from God.

The first was a red rose with a sticky note that read, "Hope you come back." Nearly eight months later, the "roses from heaven" (as I called them) came in the form of two five-petal red roses and one red rosebud.

I believed God was speaking to me through the specific colors of the roses, with the recurring theme of the red roses being *I love you.*

A couple of months passed, and the third set of roses came. This time, a five-petal pink rose and mini red rose. As was my habit each time I visited, I checked my windshield that morning, right before my sister and I went out to walk; nothing was on it. But sometime later as we returned, approaching my car from behind, I noticed something under my rear tire. It looked like plastic. I quickly moved toward it, wondering if it might be . . . and it was! There had been strong wind through the night and morning, so the roses had blown off my windshield and somehow got wedged under my tire.

Bright pink roses convey the message: *Please believe me.* With the third set of combined pink and red roses, it was as though God was communicating: *Please believe Me; I love you.*

By the way, the "Hope you come back" note with my first rose turned out to be prophetic: I came back *many* times and eventually ended up moving to the area where I received the roses! To this day, I have those dried-out roses and the sticky note—tangible reminders of divine pursuit in my wilderness season.

Divine Provision

Early on we talked about the hospitable way of the Middle East. In antiquity, hospitality was a type of "desert law." With the primary residents of the wilderness being Bedouin or nomadic, hospitality was an occasional need as they moved from place to place. It was understood that if you welcomed a stranger into your tent when they were in need, you would receive the same care when the roles were reversed. There was an expectation that hosts would provide food and water, shelter and protection for the visitor in their midst.

In the wilderness, the living God practices His own type of *desert hospitality* as He consistently provides for those journeying through.

We've witnessed this already with Hagar, who, culturally speaking, was a most unlikely candidate for special treatment. Yet by finding, seeing, and talking with this runaway maidservant who was later banished to the wilderness, the Hebrew God provided Hagar with, not only water and hope, but also a deep sense of worth—which had likely alluded her up to that point.

Elijah

God's care for Elijah was seen in the provision He made for him during his emotionally low state, as he headed towards and arrived at Mount Horeb.

One of the first provisions God made for Elijah was shade—a rare commodity in the wilderness, known as *tzel* in Hebrew. Lois Tverberg says, "In the blazing, withering heat of the desert, nothing is more welcome than the cool of the shade."[4]

Through the broom bush, God also provided a place to rest. It was here that the angel interrupted Elijah's sleep and offered nourishment—bread and water—before allowing him to rest again. The angel then supplied food and water that yielded supernatural strength for Elijah's forty-day trek to Horeb.

Both times the angel woke Elijah, the angel did so by touching him—another type of divine provision, as comfort through physical touch would have been rare for one traveling alone in the desert.

The angelic presence in the open wilderness, as well as the safety of the cave at Horeb, were divine provision of protection on Elijah's behalf.

The Israelites

God's desert hospitality was consistently experienced by the Israelites' throughout their forty years in the wilderness. Despite their grumbling and complaints, divine provision came in whatever form was needed at the time, beginning with their dramatic rescue from Pharaoh and his army at the Red Sea.

With the Egyptians closing in from behind Moses assured the people that they would see the Lord fighting for and delivering them. All night long the living God drove the sea back through a strong wind, dividing the waters and drying out the ground. As the Israelites made their way through, with walls of water on their left and right, they were encountering the divine in a way no other people had. So much so that the Egyptians insistent on pursuing them into the sea proclaimed, "'Let's get away from the Israelites! The LORD is fighting for them against Egypt'" (Ex. 14:25). When the Israelites were trapped, God provided protection and a way of escape.

The Israelites found themselves in need again as they went into the Desert of Shur. Having traveled for three days without finding water, they arrived at Marah only to discover the water was bitter and unfit to drink. As is common in wilderness regions, the need for drinkable water became an ongoing theme for the Israelites. At Marah, God, through Moses, transformed the bitter waters, making them safe and palatable to drink.

At Elim, God provided a desert oasis that included water from twelve springs and shade from seventy palm trees—believed to be a "symbolic hint that the 12 tribes and the 70 elders of Moses were coming together in rest."[5] Elim was also God's provision of a safe place to camp. The Israelites didn't just stumble upon this wilderness refuge; rather, they were led to it via divine presence in the pillar of cloud and fire.

One of the most well-known provisionary stories in the biblical narrative followed the Israelites' stint at the desert oasis, as they came to the Desert of Sin, between Elim and Sinai. In response to the Israelites' grumbling, God told Moses that He would "rain down" a type of daily bread. Each morning the people were to go out and gather just enough for that day.

For the first time in the Desert of Sin, and every morning thereafter throughout their forty wilderness years, God provided manna. This substance was so unique that even the nomadic shepherd Israelites, familiar with wilderness terrain, didn't know what it was. Along with this daily "bread from heaven," the Lord also provided meat—quail—at Sin.

Mingled in with the instructions God gave for stewarding the daily provision of manna was another type of provision, equally as unfamiliar for this nation of recently freed slaves. On the sixth day of each week, they were to gather twice as much manna, because the seventh day was to be a day of sabbath rest.

As previously observed, with 430 years of bondage being their familiar norm, the Israelites had no concept of rest. Day in and day out through their slavery in Egypt, all they knew was hard work, oppressive conditions, and impossible expectations. Through this sabbath rhythm, God was gifting the Israelites with rest; a new way of living that included trusting Him to provide enough on the sixth day to cover them while they rested on the seventh day.

According to biblical scholar Nahum Sarna, the *Talmud* reads: "The Holy One Blessed Be He said to Moses, 'I have a precious gift in My treasure house, called the Sabbath, and I desire to give it to Israel.'"[6]

Divine provision continued as the Israelites arrived at Mount Sinai. These former slaves had no concept of how to live as free people. So, God provided them with structure via *mitzvot*, Hebrew for "commandments" or "laws" related to their moral and religious conduct. The Ten Words, more commonly known as the Ten Commandments, were the first of 613 total *mitzvot*.

In yet another form of miraculous provision, the Israelites weathered their entire wilderness journey with uniquely resilient clothing and sandals that did not wear out. Ever the gracious host, God spread a generous table of provision on the Israelites' behalf—such as no other tribe or nation has experienced before or since.

It is not unusual for religious leaders to seek solitude or wilderness-type landscape to get a better grasp on their purpose. One need only look to the central figures of the Christian, Islamic, and Buddhist faiths for examples. What sets the Jewish people apart is that it was not just their leader, Moses, who experienced the wilderness years. Rather, it was the entire nation.[7]

The Israelites traversed the desert terrain communally. Together they encountered divine presence, pursuit, and provision in and through the wilderness as God traveled with and among them.

PERCEIVE ENCOUNTERS WITH THE DIVINE

As we choose to

— engage the process
— develop eyes that see
— cultivate ears that hear
— express authentic emotions

we are more readied to perceive encounters with the divine.

Questions to Consider and *Yeshiva*

1. How does the reality of divine presence distinguish you?
2. In what ways have you experienced divine presence offering you rest from striving and straining?
3. How has divine pursuit marked your wilderness seasons?
4. We've identified divine provision in and through the wilderness, but what if *the wilderness* is divine provision? How does that perspective shift your understanding of wilderness and journey?
5. Of the five postures we've discovered so far, which is the most challenging for you to implement?
   - Engage the Process
   - Develop Eyes that See
   - Cultivate Ears that Hear
   - Express Authentic Emotions
   - Perceive Encounters with the Divine

8

EMBRACE THE BECOMING

> I had escaped. But I wasn't yet free.
> —Dr. Edith Eva Eger

In our first posture, we were invited to *engage the process*. Through this sixth posture, *embrace the becoming*, we are moving from engaging to embracing—an advancement forward in our stance.

When we engage, we are choosing to participate; we are agreeing to take part. Engaging is the initial surrender or willingness to walk the path that is before us. Embracing implies a deeper level of commitment—longing for, welcoming, and receiving.

If we consider the variance in terms of relationship, to *engage* someone suggests we are talking with that individual, while *embracing* a person indicates we are hugging him or her. The latter is a closer interaction.

During my extended wilderness season, I developed a favorite word: *becoming*. I would often hear people talk about being in a "season of waiting" or "in the waiting." Those phrases grew uncomfortable for me, as they felt like a license for passivity; sitting back waiting on circumstances to change or for the desired outcome to manifest. Seeing myself as *becoming* felt like a much more active stance. I had a significant role to play in my transformation, which included embracing the season, challenging as it was, not knowing when or if it would ever end. *Becoming* became my ongoing pursuit.

Bestselling author Sue Monk Kidd says, "There is no place so alive as the edge of becoming."[1]

Becoming suggests movement.

Becoming is a continual invitation.

And here is the challenging reality: *becoming happens daily, not in a day.*

Consider this thought: in a Western, got-to-have-it-now culture, transformation—or becoming—is often what is forfeited.

When we *embrace the becoming*, we are welcoming and desirous of transformation; we are moving beyond the initial yielding. Our mindset shifts from immediate gratification or reprieve to journey and becoming.

In his popular book *As a Man Thinketh*, James Allen wrote: "Men are anxious to improve their circumstances, but are unwilling to improve themselves; they therefore remain bound."[2]

Through the lens of wilderness seasons, we might restate that as: "People are anxious to improve their circumstances by exiting the wilderness but are unwilling to improve themselves by embracing the becoming; they therefore remain stuck."

Avodah

Avodah is the Hebrew word for "work, service, or labor." It is used in Exodus 1:14, describing the Egyptians' treatment of the Israelites:

> They made their lives bitter with harsh labor [*avodah*] in brick and mortar and with all kinds of work [*avodah*] in the fields; in all their harsh labor [*avodah*] the Egyptians worked [*avodah*] them ruthlessly.

Interestingly, *avodah* can also mean *worship*, as seen here in its root form. God says to Moses, "'When you have brought the people out of Egypt, you will worship [*avad*] God on this mountain'" (Ex. 3:12). When we embrace the becoming, not only are we welcoming the hard work transformation requires, but we can also worship God in that work, with the intentional effort we put forth.

Often in wilderness seasons, the hard work of becoming is heart work; deep inner refining as a circumstance invites us to grow in self-awareness, to see who and what we really are, and respond accordingly.

Forty in the Bible

In the Bible, *forty* often signifies "change is coming," and can indicate a time of testing or preparation.

Early in the book of Genesis, we are told that the floodgates of heaven opened, causing rain to fall on the earth for forty days and forty nights. The floodwaters ushered in manifold change as God's mercy cleansed the earth from rampant corruption, wickedness, and violence.

In the book of Numbers, twelve Israelite leaders—one representative from each of the tribes—were sent to explore the land of Canaan for forty days. As they observed the land and its inhabitants, they were tested as to whether they would believe God's promise to give them possession of the land. Ten of the twelve returned with a bad report, which the Israelites responded to by weeping and complaining against Moses and Aaron. In so doing, they rejected the Promised Land and were, along with their children, fated to forty years of waiting in the wilderness—one year for each of the forty days the leaders had explored the land.

After Deborah, an Israelite prophetess and judge, led her people to victory over Sisera, there were forty years of peace in the land.

Goliath challenged the Israelites every morning and evening for forty days before David stood up to, defeated, and silenced him.

Eli, high priest of Shiloh and an Israelite judge, led Israel for forty years—as did Saul, David, and Solomon, Israel's first three kings, in that order.

As we delve into several biblical wilderness narratives of becoming, we'll see the number forty emerge as a common theme. Remember: forty often represents *change*, and the wilderness has been described as a place of *transition* (a rite of passage) and *transformation* (liminal space)—words synonymous with change.

Rabbi Sacks provides a framework for this process, which we're about to see illustrated through Moses, followed by the Israelites. He says the journey "always takes longer than you think," because it "is not just physical, a walk across the desert. It is psychological, moral, and spiritual." The journey "takes as long as the time needed for human beings to change," which "can be a very long time indeed."[3]

Moses' Middle Forty Years

Moses, commissioned by God to deliver the children of Israel from the oppression of Pharaoh and the Egyptian slave masters, experienced a significant season of becoming during his forty years of obscurity in the wilderness. If you recall, this season was preceded by forty years of lavish palace living and followed by forty years leading the Israelites through the wilderness.

We've already detailed the situational set-up that resulted in Moses fleeing to Midian, wilderness region in northwestern Arabia. A quick recap, Moses, taking justice into his own hands, murdered the Egyptian that was beating one of his own, a Hebrew. This event foreshadowed Moses as the deliverer of the Hebrew people, while also exposing his haste in handling matters his own way.

Years later, Stephen referenced this situation when he addressed the Sanhedrin, stating that Moses was forty years old when it happened. According to Stephen, Moses believed his people would recognize his actions as God using him to rescue them, but they did not see it this way.

The seeds of *mishpat*, Hebrew for "justice," had already been planted in Moses' heart. Yet refining was necessary before Moses could step into the role of deliverer God would eventually invite him to embrace.

Transformation was on Moses' horizon.

For Moses, *becoming* included being humbled as he went from prince of Egypt to tending his father-in-law's sheep in wilderness anonymity. In the palace, there were likely servants waiting to meet Moses' every need. In the hot, dry wilderness, he was doing the *avodah*—hard work—of shepherding. You may remember that the Egyptian culture Moses had grown up in looked down upon shepherds . . . the very vocation he would embody during his becoming years.

Shepherding helped Moses learn to pay attention. Honing his instinct to take a closer look at the flock he was tending prepared him to pause when he came upon the bush that was not burning up. This was just the beginning of Moses learning to steward the holy, as he would experience divine presence in manifold fashion at Mount Sinai and throughout the Israelites' wilderness years.

Moses' forty years of becoming culminated with God instructing him to return to Egypt. In describing this moment, Thomas Cahill writes: "Here is Moshe, on his face in the intense desert heat, made even fiercer by the fire before him, listening to a Voice that no one has heard since the days of Yaacov, a Voice that orders him off on an impossible mission to the very people he has been hiding from."[4]

This type directive from God—sending those who had run into the wilderness back toward the people or region they were running from—was not unusual. You may recall that God via the angel instructed Hagar to return and submit to Sarai. And God directed Elijah to return the way he had come . . . putting him back in proximity to Jezebel.

Being invited to face our fears may be a by-product of becoming through the wilderness.

After forty years in Midian, God asks Moses to take part in an adventure he could not possibly navigate in his own strength. Moses responds by questioning, "'Who am I that I should go to Pharaoh?'" (Ex. 3:11). "God's answer ignores completely Moshe's opinion of himself," observes Cahill. "For this mission will not be dependent on Moshe's abilities but on God's."[5]

Fast-forward to Exodus 14, after Pharaoh had let the Israelites go. Moses was just beginning to shepherd this nation out of captivity. We see a transformed man, faith-filled and functioning in God's strength. This time the outcome is far different, as Moses stretched out his hand over the Red Sea, watched the waters divide, and led the Israelites through on dry ground.

Humbling as the forty years of shepherding his father-in-law's sheep in the wilderness may have been, it was this season that prepared Moses for the forty years of shepherding a nation through the wilderness.

It should be noted that Moses' first forty years, growing up in Pharaoh's palace though a Hebrew by birth, were their own type of becoming. It was there that he was trained in the culture and ways of the Egyptians; experience that would be helpful years later as he interacted with Pharaoh upon returning to Egypt.

The Israelites' Forty Years

It's been said that "it took one night to get the Israelites out of Egypt; it took forty years in the desert to get Egypt out of the Israelites."[6] This alludes to becoming.

Some works of transformation can be such lengthy endeavors, the fruit isn't visible until later generations. So it was for the Israelites born into slavery in Egypt; they struggled to embrace new mindsets that would help them steward the responsibility of freedom.

"Freedom means a loss of security and predictability," explains Rabbi Sacks. "It means taking responsibility for your actions in a way a slave does not need to do." As the Israelites journeyed from Egypt to Sinai, survival was their top priority; they weren't yet thinking about freedom. But "as they were leaving Sinai on their way to the land," continues Sacks, "the full realization dawned on them of what lay ahead. As a nation, they were about to lose their childhood."[7]

Take a moment to revisit this chart comparing the mentality of a slave with the mentality of a free person.

Mentality of a Slave	Mentality of a Free Person
Strive and strain to get	Posture to receive
"Tell me what to do"	"Teach me how to live"
Blame others	Take personal responsibility
"It will always be this way"	"How can I make it better?"

Did the generation that escaped Egypt ever adopt the mentality of free people?

Not according to Thomas Cahill. He writes: "After putting up with their yammering for a couple of years, God decides to make them wander the Sinai for a full forty years before settlement in Canaan." Cahill says this would guarantee "that the whole generation of Egyptian-bred complainers will die out and be replaced by a more rugged generation, hardened by wilderness trials—born nomads who expect always to journey on."[8]

Throughout their 430 years in Egypt, the Israelites experienced exponential growth. Yet it would take forty years in the wilderness for the internal transformation needed to become a people ready to steward the land God had promised Abraham and his descendants.

As a reminder, liminal space is that "transitional state when you are in a kind of no-man's land between the old and new." Rabbi Sacks explains that the rugged, empty wilderness was, for the Israelites, "liminal space between slavery and freedom, past and future, exile and return, Egypt and the Promised Land." Sacks concludes that "*the desert is the space that makes transition and transformation possible.*"[9] In other words, the wilderness is the place of change.

Deuteronomy 8:2–4 describes what the Israelites' were being invited to experience during their wilderness years, as they learned to

shema. To hear—in particular, to listen to directives from God via Moses—and respond.

live led. God shepherded them by leading with pillars of cloud and fire. He provided ongoing guidance as long as they kept their eyes on Him and paid attention.

travel with God. He left his mountain to journey with and among them, inviting them to steward His presence in their midst.

depend on God alone. This set-apart tribe-turned-nation experienced God's ongoing provision of water, quail, manna, sandals, and clothing.

Elijah's Forty Days and Forty Nights

As we have already noted, Elijah was active in the wilderness by posturing himself to encounter the divine. In running *from* Jezebel, he chose to run *toward* Horeb, where, years before, God had revealed Himself to Moses.

The text doesn't detail what transpired during the time it took for Elijah to reach Horeb. But interestingly, the biblical author specifies it was forty days *and forty nights*—seemingly obvious information, yet powerful when we understand that forty indicates change was coming.

In the wilderness pre-Horeb, Elijah was at his lowest. The *Message* translation says, "He came to a lone broom bush and collapsed in its shade, wanting in the worst way to be done with it all—to just die: 'Enough of this, God! Take my life'" (1 Kings 19:4).

Yet, after receiving his *davar bamidbar* at Horeb, Elijah responded by carrying out the visionary directive.

Elijah's forty-day trek to Horeb was neither his starting point nor his destination; rather, it was in-between space that prepared him to encounter God at the "wasteland" in the wilderness.

Jesus' Forty Days and Forty Nights

In our next posture, we'll explore Jesus' wilderness time in-depth and discover what it yielded. For now, let's acknowledge that the apostle Matthew stated that Jesus fasted forty days *and forty nights*.

Change was coming.

Forty days without food is hard work physically, mentally, emotionally . . . in every way. Jesus embraced the becoming by allowing the Spirit to lead Him into the transformational space of wilderness, where he fasted and was subsequently tested by the devil. What resulted from this encounter was significant, as we will soon see.

My Forty-Day Fast

Months before I turned forty, I had a deep sense that God was inviting me to do a forty-day liquid-only fast—refraining from eating any solid foods during that time. My word for that calendar year was *consecration* (meaning "set apart"), and my word for thirty-nine was *embody* ("personify" or "express")—a forty-day fast at the intersection of consecration and embodiment seemed appropriate.

I've consistently fasted over the years and have encountered the divine in specific ways during and afterwards. Yet forty days was an entirely new adventure. I sensed the date I was to start, and soon after, was prompted to count the days from the end of my fast up to my birthday, which was exactly forty days! It was as though my own sort of 40/40/40 experience had been orchestrated: forty days of fasting connected to forty days leading up to my fortieth birthday.

I was stepping into a new realm of becoming and transformation. I embarked on this journey with the support and prayers of close friends. It was sacred time and space for me to embody an element of wilderness experienced by Moses, Elijah, and Jesus—who each did a type of forty-day fast in the wilderness.

What followed was forty days of physical *avodah* or hard work, as well as heart work—a pressing through for sure. I had read and heard of people who had done extended fasts and reached a point where they were having such powerful encounters with God, they felt like they could fast indefinitely. This was not my experience; every day was a new yielding to the work.

A consistent prayer of mine through the forty days was a psalm of David. I am reminded of his prayer anytime I'm at En Gedi, a waterfall-rich oasis in the Judean wilderness. David may very well have written this psalm while at En Gedi watching an ibex—a desert-dwelling deer with unique footing, able to scale cliffs and reach dangerous places.

David said God "makes me as surefooted as a deer [ibex], enabling me to stand on mountain heights" (Ps. 18:33 NLT).

Restated in prayer form: "Lord, give me feet to handle the path you've chosen for me. Change my *feet*, not my path."

In the bestselling allegorical novel by Hannah Hurnard, *Hinds' Feet on High Places*, the "hind" known as Much-Afraid was likely an ibex. Consider this exchange between Much-Afraid and the Shepherd:

> "O Shepherd. You said you would make my feet like hinds' feet and set me upon mine High Places."
>
> "Well," he answered cheerily, "the only way to develop hinds' feet is to go by the paths which the hinds use."[10]

The prophet Habakkuk made a similar declaration as David when he said: "The Sovereign LORD is my strength; he makes my feet like the feet of a deer, he enables me to tread on the heights" (Hab. 3:19).

This prayer—*"Lord, give me feet to handle the path you've chosen for me. Change my feet, not my path"*—sums up embracing the becoming. It moves us beyond yielding, to welcoming and asking God to transform us as we walk the path that has been set before us. Sometimes this requires the hard work of climbing, stepping slowly, hanging on, braving rough terrain . . . all the while choosing to press on and move forward.

As we do, we are likely to discover that transformation is experienced through the *becoming*, not in the arriving.

Questions to Consider and *Yeshiva*

1. In what ways are you forfeiting transformation by expecting quick results in the wilderness?

2. If you could have a conversation with Moses, what would you ask him about his middle forty years of becoming?

3. How might the quiet of the desert, the simplicity of shepherding, and the normalcy of having a wife and sons have been a relief for Moses, compared to life in Egypt and Pharaoh's palace?

4. Describe a wilderness season where you can see you were in transition between the old and new, the past and future. In what ways did you embrace the becoming offered by that season? How did you resist?

5. How have you been asking God to change your path or remove the challenging circumstances you are facing? What might it look like for you to ask Him to change your *feet* instead?

9

ESTABLISH HEALTHY RHYTHMS

> We are what we repeatedly do.
> —Will Durant

In challenging wilderness seasons, when we are frustrated and hurting, anxious and uncertain, we can be prone to develop *unhealthy* rhythms—that is, destructive patterns or habits. One need only view online advertisements or television commercials for the countless objects and experiences aimed at helping us numb out and avoid pain. These coping mechanisms and alternate sources of comfort can send us into an even deeper internal wilderness that we remain stuck in.

But when we choose to *establish healthy rhythms*, our seventh posture, we position ourselves for flourishing both in and out of wilderness seasons.

John Maxwell says: "Small disciplines repeated with consistency every day lead to great achievements gained slowly over time."[1] Through our wilderness lens we could restate that as: "Healthy rhythms repeated with consistency through wilderness seasons yield transformation over time."

Our rhythms matter. They position us for growth or regression, fullness or lack.

Rhythms of Rest

In a Western, got-to-get-ahead and keep-it-moving culture, the word *rest* can evoke images of laziness and falling behind.

But rest was and is meant to be a gift from God. When we establish rhythms of rest in our wilderness seasons, we are in alignment with God's original intent, a rhythm He graciously instructed the Israelites to implement as they journeyed through the wilderness.

There are more than four hundred references to *rest* in the Bible—that's more mentions than for themes such as faith, love, and joy. We tend to talk about what is meaningful to us; clearly, *rest* is a topic near and dear to the heart of God.

One of the unique differences between Western and Hebrew cultures pertains to the start of a new day. In the West, a day begins at sunrise and ends at sunset. In a Hebraic, Middle Eastern culture, the day begins at sunset, meaning, the day *begins with rest*.

Shabbat

Shabbat is the Hebrew word meaning "sabbath; to cease." Out of 613 instructions in the Mosaic covenant, the law concerning *Shabbat* is number four. The rabbis wrote more about *Shabbat* than anything else.

The first time God called something "holy" was in the wilderness at Mount Sinai, in reference to *Shabbat*. As God detailed the parameters for keeping the Sabbath, including resting and abstaining from work, He also blessed the day.

In her *Sabbath* series, Kristi McLelland says, "God rested on the seventh day after restoring creation that had been marred. His rest is a celebration of the restoration."[2] *Shabbat* is meant to be both restful and celebratory.

Susannah Heschel, daughter of scholar and author Rabbi Abraham Joshua Heschel, describes what she learned about the Sabbath from her father: "Observing the Sabbath is not only about refraining from work, but about creating *menuha*, a restfulness that is also a celebration."[3] Emphasizing the priority of *Shabbat*, Rabbi Heschel asserted, "What *we are* depends on what *the Sabbath is* to us."[4]

ESTABLISH HEALTHY RHYTHMS

Think back to Psalm 78:19, when the Israelites asked, "Can God really spread a table in the wilderness?" It was in the wilderness that God not only set a table by providing manna, a miraculous forty-year supply of bread, but He also offered the Israelites rest.

At a time when generations were approximately twelve years in length, nearly thirty-six generations of Israelites had known only slavery during their nation's four-hundred-thirty years in Egypt. They had no framework for rest. In the wilderness, by instituting the Sabbath or *Shabbat*, God *commanded* the Israelites to rest—it was not a suggestion. And He was gracious to give them specific instructions for how to implement this new rhythm.

Shabbat was given to an entire nation, not an individual. It was and is meant to be a communal celebration of the restoration. Thomas Cahill says: "The Sabbath is surely one of the simplest and sanest recommendations any god has ever made."[5]

Shabbat is God inviting us to experience *shalom*: wholeness, flourishing, and delight. It's an opportunity for a rhythm of rest that produces deep internal peace. *Shabbat* is when crooked is made straight, sick is made well, broken is made whole—as demonstrated through Jesus, who had a pattern of healing on *Shabbat*.

According to Isaiah 58, honoring the Sabbath carries a promise:

> "If you watch your step on the Sabbath and don't use my holy day for personal advantage, if you treat the Sabbath as a day of joy, God's holy day as a celebration, if you honor it by refusing 'business as usual,' making money, running here and there—*then you'll be free to enjoy God!*" (vv. 13–14 MSG, emphasis added)

Sabbath is "the day when we stop thinking of the *price* of things and focus instead on the *value* of things," says Rabbi Sacks. "On Shabbat we can't buy or sell. We can't work or pay others to work for us. It's the day dedicated to the celebration of the things that have value but no price."[6] *Shabbat* invites us to slow down and enjoy who and what matters.

In her critically acclaimed *Leaving Church*, Barbara Brown Taylor says: "Stop for one whole day every week, and you will remember what it means to be created in the image of God, who rested on the seventh day not from weariness but from complete freedom." She continues with a hope-filled invitation: "The clear promise is that those who rest like God find themselves free like God, no longer slaves to the thousand compulsions that send others rushing toward their graves.[7]

While the initial command to honor the Sabbath was issued for the seventh day, in the book of Hebrews, the biblical author speaks of a Sabbath-rest that is ever available. We are invited to intentionally enter that rest.

Through our previous posture, *embrace the becoming*, we saw how transformation requires hard work or *avodah*. Establishing a healthy rhythm of rest supports us in the *avodah*.

Rhythms of a Rabbi

In Matthew 4, we see Jesus being led or compelled into the wilderness by the Spirit of God. This was likely something Jesus knew was coming. He had just been baptized and, in the presence of three witnesses—John the Baptist, God the Father, and the Holy Spirit—had received His rabbinic authority.

With a Hebraic understanding that "the word of the Lord came to" those whom God had chosen, it was probable Jesus anticipated that He was about to receive His *davar bamidbar*—His word in the wilderness. As a rabbi this word would then become His *halakha*, the way in which He and His followers would walk and live.

After His time of testing in the wilderness, Jesus called His first disciples, began healing the sick, and delivered His Sermon on the Mount (see Matthew 5–7), which is thought to be the word He received in the wilderness.

As we take a closer look at Jesus' forty days of fasting in the wilderness, as well as His interaction with the devil, we see specific actions of Rabbi Jesus *in* the wilderness, which He would carry with Him *outside* the wilderness; they became rhythms in His years of ministry. Jesus postured Himself in ways we can emulate.

1. *He allowed Himself to be led.* This would also be true during His years of ministry, about which Jesus said, "I do nothing on my own but speak just what the Father has taught me" (John 8:28).

2. *He yielded to testing.* According to the *NIV First-Century Study Bible*, "The Greek word *peirazo* also means *test*. In the Hebrew Bible, God tested his servants (see Ge 22:1; Dt 8:2). The external wilderness tested the state of the heart, revealing that the inner battle was the true battle."[8]

    Referring to Jesus, Hebrews 4:15 says: "This High Priest of ours understands our weaknesses, for he faced all of the same testings we do, yet he did not sin" (NLT).

3. *He practiced fasting.* Throughout His ministry Jesus modeled and taught the discipline of fasting, which was implied by His statement "When you fast," in Matthew 6:16.

    Tertullian, who has been called "the father of Latin Christianity" and "the founder of Western theology," believed it was common for early Christians to fast for a time after they were baptized, thus following the pattern of Jesus.

    Fasting slows us down and breaks our rhythms of normalcy, as the time regularly devoted to eating is instead given to solitude and contemplation.

4. *He took time for the matter at hand.* Jesus' prolonged fast prepared Him for the wilderness test. He wasn't in a hurry, as would also be the case throughout His ministry.

    "Food tasted better at the pace he set. Stories lasted longer. Talk went deeper," says Barbara Brown Taylor, as she paints a picture of Jesus' willingness to linger. "While many of his present-day admirers pay close attention to what he said and did, they pay less attention to the pace at which he did it. Jesus . . . took his sweet time."[9]

5. *He answered the challenger with the Word of God.* Rabbi Jesus would have known Torah and likely even had it all memorized. He responded to each of the devil's tests with passages from Deuteronomy, all of which were given to the Israelites when they were tested in the wilderness.

    Throughout Jesus' ministry, it was often the religious leaders—such as the Pharisees, chief priests, and Sanhedrin—who attempted to trap or test Him. Jesus responded to them as He did to Satan, by quoting Scripture (see Matt. 26:59-64).

6. *He focused on the bigger picture and purpose.* With the cross ever in mind, even though Jesus was in a physically weakened state, He didn't fall for the counterfeit options—power and fame, that Satan offered to temporarily satisfy His appetite. Jesus demonstrated much humility in *allowing* Himself to be tested, goaded, and mocked by the devil.

   The wilderness was preparation for Gethsemane on the horizon. It was there that Jesus would describe his soul as being "'overwhelmed with sorrow to the point of death'" (Matt. 26:38). Multiple times He asked God to take away this cup of suffering.

   Jesus' self-denial through His wilderness test readied Him for His Gethsemane test. The disciples, whom Jesus had asked to keep watch with Him and pray, had not yet faced similar testing and preparation. When Jesus needed them most, they kept falling asleep.

7. *He prioritized solitude.* Throughout Jesus' ministry, as He became more and more known, taking time to be alone was essential.

   After Jesus heard about John the Baptist's death, "he withdrew by boat privately to a solitary place" (Matt. 14:13). As previously mentioned, in the Greek, the phrase "solitary place" is *eremos topos* and can imply a desolate desert or wilderness region. Jesus no doubt went there requesting comfort from His Father both for John's disciples and for Himself.

   Following the feeding of the five thousand, Jesus again sought time alone. After dismissing the crowd, He went up on a mountainside to pray, and was there alone later that night.

   On another occasion, after healing many people and casting out demons, he got up "very early in the morning, while it was still dark, . . . left the house and went off to a solitary place, where he prayed" (Mark 1:35).

   In fact, "Jesus often withdrew to the wilderness for prayer" (Luke 5:16 NLT). For Jesus, there was something comforting and inviting about the desolate and lonely places. I wonder if each time He went alone to *eremos topos*, He was reminded of His forty-day wilderness fast. And if reflecting back on that time of overcoming "the Test" encouraged and empowered Him for the multitudes clamoring to be touched by Him or the religious leaders eager to trap Him.

8. *He allowed Himself to be tended to.* Following the wilderness test, the devil left, and angels came to Jesus' aid.

   After His crucifixion, many women, including Mary Magdalene and Mary the mother of James and Joseph, came to take care of Him. Joseph of Arimathea wrapped Jesus' body in a fresh linen cloth and placed it in his tomb.

These actions chosen by Rabbi Jesus while *in* the wilderness became healthy rhythms throughout His ministry years.

Rhythms of Relationship

"The most significant factor in any person's environment is the people," asserts John Maxwell in *The 15 Invaluable Laws of Growth*. "So think long and hard about who you're spending the most time with, for wherever they are headed, so are you."[10] Proverbs 13:20 affirms this truth: "Walk with the wise and become wise, for a companion of fools suffers harm."

Who we allow ourselves to be influenced by plays a key role in our mindset and actions. Harvard social psychologist Dr. David McClelland says, "The people with whom you associate are called your 'reference' group; and these people determine as much as 95% of your success or failure in life."[11] Author, psychologist, and leadership expert Dr. Henry Cloud says: "Your own performance is either improved or diminished by the other people in your scenario."[12]

In wilderness seasons when we are facing difficulties, navigating heightened emotions, and experiencing fear and uncertainty, whom we choose to surround ourselves with directly impacts our outlook towards and stewardship of our wilderness time.

Numbers 11 illustrates this well. The Israelites' wilderness journey was a different kind of work than the labor they had been accustomed to during their years of slavery in Egypt. Where there was already a propensity to complain, the "foreign rabble" influenced the Israelites to despise their daily manna and desire the delicacies they'd had in Egypt—where they'd been oppressed and burdened, a reality they seemed to have forgotten.

Rhythms of Release

Wilderness seasons can be intense, painful, and challenging—and can push us to our max. Establishing healthy rhythms of release is another key to stewarding wilderness seasons well. These rhythms are constructive avenues for releasing pent-up energy, taking a mental break, and expressing emotions.

Rhythms of release may overlap with your rhythms of rest and can include, but are not limited to, activities such as walking, running, golfing, gardening, fishing, hiking, playing a musical instrument, painting, cooking—the options are endless! In choosing a healthy rhythm of release, understand that what works well for someone else may not be your ideal.

My primary rhythm of release during my extended wilderness season was to walk, look, and listen. On days where I felt like I was never going to move beyond my current circumstances, I would take a walk—sometimes hours long—and move my body, which calmed my heart and mind. With my eyes eager to see and my ears open to hear and respond, I *expected* to encounter the divine. Step after step I felt a supernatural strength giving me feet for the path I had been invited to walk.

Rabbis and sages consider walking to be a rhythm that allows for processing through a challenging teaching that's been heard and received. In Jesus' day, it would have been the norm to see a rabbi and *talmidim* walking together, by discussing what they were learning through impassioned *yeshiva*.

If you don't yet have a rhythm of release and aren't sure where to start, lace up your shoes and go for a walk. "Not everyone is able to walk, but most people can, which makes walking one of the most easily available spiritual practices of all," says Barbara Brown Taylor.[13]

Whether its hitting or kicking a punching bag, riding horses, or playing ping pong, healthy rhythms of release contribute significantly to our wilderness wellbeing.

Rhythms of Recording

As noted in an earlier posture, the Hebrews are a culture of the ear—a *hearing* culture. It was not uncommon for young Hebrew boys to memorize entire portions of the Torah. Through oral tradition that involved repeating and recording, they passed down stories we still read thousands of years later.

For years I've thought of myself as a scribe, one who records what I see and hear. This rhythm, which began in my prolonged wilderness season, has helped me remember important information to a degree that often causes people to ask how I'm able to so easily recall significant dates and times.

It may seem a bit old-fashioned, but I believe noteworthy moments should be captured through handwritten script. Research supports that writing by hand allows us to think more clearly about the information being recorded. It encourages the expansion of thoughts and helps us make connections between them. When we record by hand, we are engaging different senses simply by holding and moving a pen or pencil, feeling the paper beneath our hand, and using our mind to direct the movement of our writing tool.

Understandably, recording by hand isn't always possible in a moment. What's important is being ready to capture meaningful thoughts and occurrences. When I go out to walk, look, and listen, I'll silence the ringer on my phone, yet carry it with me so I can record a note if something surfaces during that time. Inevitably, though, I'll transport notes from my phone into a handwritten journal.

With ever-evolving technology, new methods of recording continue to emerge. However we go about it, rhythms of recording directly set us up for *rhythms of remembering*, which we will cover in-depth in our ninth posture.

Some of the final words uttered by Jewish historian Simon Dubnow, before he was killed by the Nazi regime during the Holocaust, capture the weight of recording to preserve memory. Said Dubnow, "Keep writing Jews, keep writing."[14] Or, as it reads in Yiddish, "Jews, write and record."

Questions to Consider and *Yeshiva*

1. What "small disciplines" or healthy rhythms are you implementing and maintaining throughout your wilderness season?

2. What *unhealthy* rhythms do you need to replace with more life-giving alternatives?

3. What are your current rhythms of rest?

4. What challenges do you experience choosing self-denial in a Western culture patterned after the Hellenistic mindset: *If it tastes good eat it. If it feels good do it. if it looks good watch it*?

5. Who are you *most* connected to? Who do you need to be *better* connected to, so you can thrive through the wilderness?

6. What are your rhythms of release? How do you feel during and after these activities?

7. Which of the following rhythms do you need to focus on developing?
    - Rhythms of Rest
    - Rhythms of a Rabbi
    - Rhythms of Relationship
    - Rhythms of Release
    - Rhythms of Recording

10

MAKE THE MOST OF DELAYS AND DETOURS

> There is a long way which is short
> and a short way which is long.
> —*Babylonian Talmud*, Tractate Eruvin 53b

During extended wilderness seasons, when we're weary and ready for circumstantial change, it can be common to question,

How much longer?
Am I headed in the right direction?
Is it always going to be this way?
Did I do something wrong?
When will this end?

Delays can be maddening when our anticipated arrival at a destination is hindered. Detours are frustrating when our preferred route is interrupted, and our progress is slowed down. As we navigate the often-uncertain pathways characteristic of wilderness seasons, we always get to choose whether we will *make the most of delays and detours*.

Sometimes the delays are a direct result of our choices, as it was for the children of Israel. What should have been an eleven-day trip from Horeb to Kadesh Barnea, the southern border of the Promised Land, became forty years of wilderness waiting and desert dwelling. Yet even through their disobedience and the subsequent delays and detours, God graciously went before them, looking for safe places for them to camp, and guiding them in which way to go.

Sabab

The Hebrew word *sabab* means "to go around" or "to turn about," and is the foundation for our eighth posture. We see this word and concept in Deuteronomy 2, as Moses recounted for the Israelites the Lord's words of guidance: "'You have made your way around [*sabab*] this hill country long enough; now turn north'" (v. 3).

You may recall that God didn't lead the Israelites on the shorter coastal route to the Promised Land, which would have taken them directly through Philistine territory. God knew that if they were faced with battling the warrior sea people so soon after escaping Egypt, they were prone to return. "So," Exodus 13:18 says, "God led them in a roundabout [*sabab*] way through the wilderness toward the Red Sea" (NLT).

A "Roundabout Way"

For hundreds of years, the Israelites had been in a circumstantial wilderness as slaves to Pharaoh. Consistent with the Hebrew God's redemptive nature, He used their time in Egypt to grow the family of Jacob (whose name God changed to "Israel") into a rapidly expanding nation. Genesis 46:27 tells us that "the members of Jacob's family, which went to Egypt, were seventy in all." According to Exodus 12, about six hundred thousand men came out of Egypt, not including women and children.

Seventy men went in; six hundred thousand men came out. Whether those amounts are literal or symbolic, the point is that *many* more Israelites exited Egypt than had gone in over four centuries earlier. The Israelites had become so fruitful and numerous that the land was filled with them.

While their liberation happened overnight, maturation and transformation were going to take time. So God rescued them and then He led them in *a roundabout way*—a deliberately longer route through the wilderness.

It's been accurately said that "No one heals in a straight line."[1] We could restate that as: "No one *becomes* or *transforms* by a direct route"— which correlates with the Middle Eastern mindset of journey and process.

Consider the meanings of *sabab*. To go around. To turn about. A roundabout way. Going around in circles. This may be what we, too, experience through delays and detours in our wilderness seasons.

God took the children of Israel on a circuitous route because in their downtrodden state, still carrying the mindset of slaves, He saw what they couldn't see. Says Thomas Cahill: "God is apparently afraid that this people he has decided to champion have little fortitude and may use any calamity as an excuse to return to the security of their previous servitude."[2]

All the Israelites knew was *escape*; it was the theme of their narrative as they had escaped from Pharaoh's arrogance and brutality, oppressive taskmasters, and the obstacle of the Red Sea. But *freedom* was their destiny. The "roundabout way," fraught with delays and detours, invited them to learn a new *halakha*; a new way of walking and living.

"Like an Army Ready for Battle"

The Israelites were a weakened, demoralized people who had not tasted freedom in nearly thirty-six generations. Yet Exodus 13:18 says something peculiar: "The Israelites left Egypt like an army ready for battle."

Forty years into their future, God saw a nation that would have to go in and *possess* the good land He was bringing them into, which would include fighting the "ites" currently inhabiting it. Liminal space and place were needed to transform them into a people ready to take hold of the Promised Land and steward the responsibility of freedom.

God saw the Israelites as they were, yet He also saw who they were *becoming*: an army ready for battle. By detouring them through the wilderness, God was protecting the Israelites from weaknesses they didn't yet have the capacity to see in themselves.

In his philosophical work *The Guide for the Perplexed*, the Jewish philosopher Maimonides writes: "It was the result of God's wisdom that the Israelites were led about in the wilderness until they acquired courage. Besides," continues the prolific Torah scholar, "another generation arose during the wanderings, that had not been accustomed to degradation and slavery."[3]

Desert People

We tend to be more "at home" or relaxed when in the landscape we're accustomed to. People who grow up wearing flip-flops and surfing the waters of sunny California beaches may struggle to adapt to the harsh winter elements of the Midwest, with its heavy snowfall and subzero temperatures. We acclimate toward the familiar; it's comfortable and even *comforting* for us.

The same was true for the Philistines and the Israelites. The Philistines were seamen, a maritime or water people who worshipped Dagon, the scaly, fishlike water god. The Mediterranean Sea provided the western border of Philistine territory.

In contrast, the Israelites were land or desert people also known as *Hapiru*, meaning the "Dusty Ones" from the mountains and deserts. Bodies of water were not a cultural norm or a leisurely experience for the Hebrews. To this day, there are not cottages or homes along the shores of the Galilee; the locals still don't build by water. Other than tourists out for a boat ride, the water lacks the presence of people.

In guiding the Israelites through the wilderness, God was graciously detouring them by way of an avenue they were more comfortable with. Yet their journey began with God leading them straight *toward* the Red Sea, an obstacle they would have been terrified to face.

In a 2012 dialogue between Rabbi Jonathan Sacks and evolutionary biologist Richard Dawkins at the BBC RE:Think Festival, Rabbi Sacks describes the scenario that unfolded at the Red Sea: "We have a picture of the weakest of the weak, a group of escaping slaves, and a group of the strongest of the strong." Rabbi Sacks explains that "the Egypt of the Pharaohs was the longest lived and greatest empire the world has ever known." Lasting 3,000 years, it was at its zenith during the time of Rameses II. With access to the horse-drawn chariot, the Egyptian military was formidable indeed.[4]

The "weakest of the weak"—the Israelites—were trapped, with Pharaoh and the Egyptian charioteers closing in from behind and the Red Sea hindering their forward progress. If we were to get into the mind of an ancient Hebrew, we would sense their deep fear of water; to them, water represented chaos or the abyss.

In her *Israel* series, Kristi McLelland says, "Part of what the Israelites lost in their years of slavery was their ability to imagine God."[5] In splitting the Red Sea, the God of Abraham, Isaac, and Jacob displayed mastery over the chaos, reshaping the Israelites' understanding of Him.

This cultural insight helps us better grasp the disciples' awe and astonishment when Jesus calmed the stormy sea and walked on the water. As the living God had done hundreds of years prior on their ancestors' behalf, so their rabbi was demonstrating His mastery over the chaos. For the Hebrews, this was revolutionary.

Beautiful in Form, Barren in Function

At the start of our journey together, we identified several fundamental differences between Western and Middle Eastern cultures. A primary variance is that Westerners tend to value *form*—how an object or person looks, while Middle Easterners value *function*—what a person or thing does. This is vividly illustrated in the cultural expectations placed on women.

As noted earlier, in antiquity, a woman's worth was in her womb—her *function*. So much so that "in a world starving for children," writes Liora Ravid, "it was not logical to 'waste' the womb of a fertile woman who could bear healthy children, just because she was blind, crippled, or born with a harelip that ruined her face." Ravid concludes "that in biblical times, a lame but fertile concubine was worth more than a senior wife who was beautiful but barren."[6]

In Western cultures, a woman's outward appearance, or *form*, is prioritized. Endless options for image maintenance contribute to a thriving industry centered around women attaining their desired or expected form.

Because the Bible was written by Middle Easterners living within a function-over-form framework, when a person's *form* is mentioned, it is purposeful. We should take notice because a necessary detail is being given to help us understand the greater narrative.

With that cultural context in mind, what becomes intriguing is that the form, or beauty, of three of the four Hebrew matriarchs—Sarai, Rebekah, and Rachel—is explicitly stated by the biblical author. What's even more fascinating is that each of these matriarchs was infertile; they were *beautiful but barren*, having lovely form in a culture that valued function.

As we are about to see, the *wilderness of waiting* endured by each of these women was the "roundabout way" by which God chose to grow the Hebrew tribe.

Sarai

In introducing Sarai, wife of Abram, the biblical author states that she was "unable to become pregnant and had no children" (Gen. 11:30 NLT). When Abram and Sarai went to Egypt to avoid the famine in Canaan, everyone noticed Sarai's beauty—so much so that the palace officials took her to Pharaoh.

Because of Sarai, Pharaoh gave Abram many gifts, including male and female servants. As previously mentioned, scholars believe this is when Hagar was added to Abram and Sarai's household. The Egyptian maidservant who would effortlessly get pregnant was likely received as a by-product of Sarai's external beauty. Cultural tension runs deep in this narrative.

The description of Sarai as unable to conceive and exceptionally beautiful would have resonated with ancient audiences. Women would have *felt* Sarai's shame while men may have thought, *What a shame.*

Sarah's wilderness of waiting lasted until she was ninety years old, when, finally, she gave birth to Isaac. The "roundabout way" Sarah traversed was one of the longest delay-filled paths recorded in the biblical narrative.

Rebekah

The next Hebrew matriarch, Rebekah, is also introduced with attention given to her "stunningly beautiful" form (Gen. 24:16 MSG). Rebekah married Isaac when he was forty years old. Before having Esau and Jacob, she experienced twenty years of barrenness—a circuitous route to motherhood that no doubt felt like an eternity.

Having left her immediate family in northwestern Mesopotamia and moved to the Negev to marry Isaac, Rebekah weathered this wilderness of waiting far from the comfort and safety of home. The gravity of her decision to leave is felt through this excerpt from the *Cultural Backgrounds Study Bible*: "Until a woman conceived and bore a child to her new family, her status within the family was tenuous, and the proximity of her father's family would have been a strong motivator for her husband not to mistreat her or discard her."[7]

With the added pressure of being married to the covenant son, three to four years of childlessness would have been challenging enough. *Twenty years* of hope deferred was a weighty wilderness to walk through.

Leah and Rachel

Rebekah was followed by Leah and Rachel, sister-wives of Jacob and last in the matriarchal line. Leah, the older sister, is described as "tender eyed" (Gen. 29:17 KJV), a cultural idiom hinting that something may have been wrong with her appearance—or that she was prone to cry, as believed by other scholars. Rachel, on the other hand, is said to have been beautiful with a lovely figure—and Jacob was in love with her.

Because Leah was unloved, God intervened and enabled her to conceive. What was lacking in Leah's *form* was more than made up for by her *function*. Thus, her position in Jacob's household was secure.

While Jacob's love for Rachel is repeatedly noted, tensions escalated over her barrenness, a condition her beautiful form could not assuage. It wasn't until after Leah had six sons and a daughter that the burden of barrenness finally lifted for Rachel. This "roundabout way" was wrought with disgrace and friction.

The importance of function over form is evident even in how the sister-wives were stewarded after death. Rachel died giving birth to her second son and was buried along the road to Ephraim. If Jacob had wanted to bury her with the rest of the family at Machpelah in Hebron, it would have only taken him a day's walk to transport her there.

This may not seem significant until we consider Jacob's request, years later, as he gathered his sons around his deathbed in Egypt. Jacob instructed them to carry his bones hundreds of miles from Egypt back to Machpelah. He said, "There Abraham and his wife Sarah are buried.

There Isaac and his wife, Rebekah, are buried. And there I buried Leah" (Gen. 49:31). Jacob was buried with his *fertile* wife, whose final resting place was in the tomb of the patriarchs and matriarchs.

Barren in the Barren

This painful pattern of prolonged physical barrenness mirrored the desolate wilderness regions the matriarchs lived in and journeyed through. Each of these women's personal *wilderness of waiting*, was, in the grander scheme, God's "roundabout way" to build a new tribe. These desert dwellers had barren beginnings.

This should prompt us to ask: *Why would God do it like that? What was the purpose of the delays and detours?*

"I Will"

Clues are found in God's promises to Abraham throughout the book of Genesis. God says:

> "I will make you into a great nation, and I will bless you; I will make your name great" (12:2).

> "I will make a covenant with you, by which I will guarantee to give you countless descendants" (17:2 NLT).

> "I will make you extremely fruitful. . . I will confirm my covenant with you and your descendants after you, from generation to generation" (17:6–7 NLT).

> "I will bless [Sarah] and give you a son from her! Yes, I will bless her richly, and she will become the mother of many nations" (17:16 NLT).

> "I will certainly bless you. I will multiply your descendants beyond number, like the stars in the sky and the sand on the seashore" (22:17 NLT).

Barrenness was an opportunity for the living God to do the very thing He had repeatedly promised to do. Through Sarah, Rebekah, and Rachel, we see evidence that God is not just a covenant-maker, He is also a covenant-keeper. No matter how long the delay between promise and fulfillment, no matter how painful the detour, God always follows through.

Isaac, the promised son, was born in his parents' old age. Then came Jacob, whose name God would change to *Israel*, meaning "one who wrestles with God." Jacob's twelve sons became the twelve tribes of Israel.

The God of the Hebrews sees time differently than we often do. Delays and detours are well-worn pathways on the road to transformation.

Transformation Is the Priority

Understanding the function of delays and detours in wilderness seasons helps provide meaning and purpose.

In Deuteronomy 8, Moses called the Israelites to move forward by looking back at what God had done for them. In the early days of their forty-year *wilderness of waiting*, God allowed them to feel the discomfort and fear attached to not having food readily available. After they experienced hunger, He fed them. Their comfort was not His priority; their transformation was.

God didn't feed them with familiar food; rather, He provided "a food previously unknown" to them or their ancestors—so mysterious that when they saw it, they asked, "What is it?" Why would God do this? Why not give them foods they were accustomed to . . . foods they had a taste for?

Eating this food, this "manna" as they called it, required trusting God with the unknown. The wilderness, with all its delays and detours, is full of uncertainties. Eating manna every day for forty years was a daily reminder that they didn't live on bread alone. Their greatest source of nourishment were the words, the *devarim*, that came from the mouth of the living God.

In *Man's Search for Meaning*, Holocaust survivor and logotherapy founder Victor Frankl writes: "When we are no longer able to change a situation, we are challenged to change ourselves."[8] The Israelites could not change the type of food God chose to provide, nor could they change the duration of their wilderness years. What they *could* change was how they would respond.

Liberation happened overnight, but maturation came over time. The Israelites' wilderness years illustrate that *freedom is gained daily, not in a day*. It took forty years in the desert to get the slave mentality learned in Egypt out of the Israelites. God does not seem overly concerned with us reaching our desired destination as quickly as possible. The roundabout way, including its delays and detours, is often the transformational path.

Gratitude for Delays and Detours

Over the course of my eleven-year wilderness season, I experienced no less than fourteen detours, professionally speaking, between organizations I worked for or with, and business ventures I was part of. There were many moments when I would think, *What's the point of this?* Or I would experience what became a familiar feeling of being "led but lost"—knowing deep down that my steps were being guided, yet unable to recognize how each individual step related to the overall pathway of my life.

Looking back, I see with gratitude how every delay and detour was necessary for my transformation and growth. Some were enjoyable; others were painful and hard to endure. As I made the most of the delays and detours, my self-awareness grew, unwanted baggage was discarded, and healthier ways were embraced.

I have yet to meet a person who regrets choosing to make the most of delays and detours. Rather, there is gratitude for the necessary growth and change they were being invited into, even if it came via a path they would not have originally chosen to walk.

Questions to Consider and *Yeshiva*

1. Describe a scenario where you recognize God saw who you were becoming and invited you into a wilderness season that would shape you into that person.

2. As you reflect on your wilderness seasons, are there any frustrating delays and detours that you now see were God protecting you from returning to an unhealthy familiar?

3. In what ways might you be missing what God is trying to show you about Himself because you are so focused on the obstacle—the uncomfortable scenario—you are facing?

4. In your wilderness seasons, how has God invited you to lean into the unfamiliar?

5. Describe a *wilderness of waiting* you have experienced. How did you encounter the divine through that season?

6. How has God allowed you to "go hungry" in wilderness seasons so He could feed you a new type of food?

7. What do you hunger for in wilderness seasons, that only the living God can satisfy?

11

EMBODY THE WILDERNESS

> The longer you can look back, the further you can see forward.
> —Winston Churchill

When we *embody the wilderness*, our ninth posture, we represent or personify what we have become as we've chosen to walk the path before us.

We are different people than when we first entered the wilderness. No longer clamoring to get out, we're more settled. Perhaps even calm in the chaos.

We've embraced the Middle Eastern mindset of journey. We're grateful for the work the wilderness has done in us as we are being transformed.

By determining to embody the wilderness, we have taken on the attitude of *How can we keep the wilderness in us?* instead of *How fast can we escape?*

Zakhar

Zakhar comes from the Hebrew verb *Z-KH-R*, meaning "remember." Moses used *zakhar* twenty-one times in the book of Deuteronomy alone. Repeatedly, he exhorted the Israelites to remember; from their slavery in Egypt and the divine deliverance they experienced, to God leading them through the wilderness for forty years. Moses even urged the Israelites to remember how they had provoked the Lord's anger.

Choosing to consistently *zakhar*, or maintain a rhythm of remembering, is foundational for embodying the wilderness. Lois Tverberg describes how the English language defines *remember* solely through the process of "recalling memories and bringing ideas into our thoughts." To *forget*, then, is to *not* be able to recall a particular memory. Tverberg says, "Both words are concerned entirely with mental activity—whether or not information is present." In contrast, the Hebrew verb *zakhar* also encompasses the actions one takes in response to remembering.[1]

Just as there is no word for "obey" in biblical Hebrew, neither is there a word for "history." The closest is *zakhor*, which means "memory." From a Jewish perspective, history and memory are inherently distinct. History has been described as "his story," a description of events that happened to some other person at some other time. Memory, on the other hand, is "my story;" internalizing the past so that it becomes part of my identity. While history tells us what happened, memory tells us who we are.[2]

Before we look more closely at *zakhar*, let's take a few minutes to consider further context that will help us better grasp the importance of remembering as it relates to embodying the wilderness.

The Land of Milk and Honey

During Moses' encounter with the Lord at Mount Horeb, God told Moses that He had seen the misery of the Hebrew people and had heard them crying out in response to their suffering. Concerned, God promised to rescue them from the Egyptians and bring them into a land flowing with milk and honey.

The *land of milk* refers to wilderness, or *midbar* region, where shepherds tend their herds of sheep and goats to produce milk and cheese products. To survive in the land of milk, we need God to provide water, bread, and shade.

The *land of honey* includes the agriculturally rich farmland comprised of coastal plain and mountains, where farmers live. The name derives from honeybees that make honey from the flowers of the pomegranates, grapes, figs, and olives, as well as date honey from date palms.

As part of an onsite lesson in Israel's Negev desert, teacher Ray Vander

Laan walks through a powerful visual of the land of milk. He talks about the rarity, in biblical days up to the present, of seeing flocks of sheep in the farm country. Due to the shortage of farmland, farmers would intentionally keep the shepherds out as much as possible because "you don't want sheep where you can farm." As Vander Laan points to the rocky, rugged wilderness terrain, he says, "*This* is the land of the shepherd"—a reality that often surprises Westerners, who have an altogether different mental picture of what "green pastures" where shepherds lead their sheep look like.[3]

The *land of milk and honey* is the place where shepherds and farmers can exist next to and cooperate with each other, such as Tekoa, where the prophet Amos was from. Amos was unique in that he functioned as both shepherd and farmer.

With that foundational understanding of the land of milk and honey—the good and spacious land God was sending the Israelites into—let's look at some features of the wilderness that will help us gain clarity.

Flash Floods

Oftentimes when we think about potential dangers in the wilderness, the primary ones that come to mind are dehydration and sun exposure. Yet surprisingly, the biggest threat in the wilderness is flash floods.

It rains in the mountains, or land of honey, up to forty inches per year, all in a short period of time; typically, December through February. The mountains can't handle that much rain in such a quick stretch. Excess water runs down the mountains and ultimately into the desert, which can result in a flash flood.

In wilderness-related conversations with Israeli archaeologist Dr. Gabi Barkay, he referenced Herod's genius at using these floods to his advantage by diverting water into his palace fortresses in the Judean wilderness. Nomadic desert dwellers still practice this today, redirecting water into cisterns and reservoirs to be used as needed.

It's been said that Bedouins can *smell* rain forty miles away. They also have a heightened ability to hear rain. Bedouin shepherdesses will stand with the end of a barrel on a wire and hit it with an iron bar, listening for the sound in the distance . . . the sound that tells them to get out of danger's way because it is raining somewhere. Bedouins know that once they *hear* the water, if they're not in a safe place, death is imminent.

Wadi

The waters from a flash flood collect in a *wadi*, Arabic for a vast canyon or dry wilderness riverbed. Wadis can accumulate an enormous amount of water and present the most dangerous threat during springtime. If you're in a wadi when it floods, you will most likely die. David was referencing a wadi in Psalm 23 when he mentioned walking through "the valley of the shadow of death."

Wilderness hikers get so hot and thirsty that when they see water at the bottom of a wadi and crouch down to drink it, they risk being surprised and killed by an incoming flood. It may be a hot, cloudless day, but in a moment, seventy feet of water will come through and they'll be washed away.

Shepherds and Still Water

In the wilderness, "still water" is water that originated from a spring or other safe source. You can get down on your hands and knees to drink still water without being at risk of death by a flash flood.

The other type water found in the wilderness may look just as good and fresh as still water, but if you bend down to drink it, you could face sudden death—as it may be leftover floodwater in a location prone to another flash flood hitting swiftly and without warning.

David spoke of quiet or *still water*, and the role of a shepherd. He said: "The LORD is my shepherd, I lack nothing. He makes me lie down in green pastures, he leads me beside quiet [*menuha*] waters" (Ps. 23:1-2). You may recall the Hebrew word *menuha*—meaning "restful"—from our section on rhythms of rest. Good shepherds lead their sheep to calming, safe waters.

In wilderness seasons, when the temptation to drink from *unsafe* waters, or engage in harmful behaviors to numb our way through, is intensified, we would be wise to heed the voice of our Shepherd. He promises to guide us always; to satisfy our needs through dry desert places; to strengthen and restore us (see Is. 58:11). Our wilderness wellbeing often depends on how closely we stay to the Shepherd as we are being led along the path.

Miry Clay

After the waters from a flash flood recede, the remnant is miry clay, a sticky mud six to eight inches deep, that comes up over the ankles.

In Psalm 40, David talks about God lifting him out of the slimy pit—or the mud and mire—and setting his feet on a rock. David is painting a picture of desperation and rescue; being stuck in a *wadi* when a flash flood is coming. There is nothing he can do but cry out to God for help.

Ever-present through our wilderness seasons, our Good Shepherd leads us to safe waters, hears our cry for help, and sets our feet on firm places.

Shakach

What does all this context have to do with remembering and embodying the wilderness?

While the biggest danger in a literal wilderness is being in a *wadi* and getting caught off guard by a flash flood, as we think about *emerging from* wilderness seasons, the most prominent danger is forgetting the Lord.

Moses issued the warning "do not forget" fourteen times in Deuteronomy. *Shakach*, Hebrew for "forget," can also mean "ignore."

In Deuteronomy 6, Moses depicted a coming scenario that could lull the Israelites to sleep if they did not practice a rhythm of remembering. When God brought them into the land, and they enjoyed living in cities and homes they did not build, drinking water from cisterns they did not dig, and eating from vineyards and trees they did not plant . . . it was then that they must be mindful not to forget the Lord.

Later, in Deuteronomy 8, Moses described the lush land the Israelites were preparing to enter. It would have streams and overflowing springs; an ample food supply, including wheat and barley, fig trees and vines, pomegranates, olive oil, honey, and bread. The land would be teeming with natural resources like iron and copper. Moses again spoke cautionary words about dwelling in this long-awaited land: "When you have eaten and are satisfied, praise the Lord your God for the good land he has given you. Be careful that you do not forget the Lord your God" (vv. 10-11).

Moses further warned that when they felt the pleasure of increase and abundance, they would be more prone to forget the Lord, which would ultimately destroy them. He implored the Israelites to remember God as the one who had given them the ability to produce wealth.

Like the Israelites, for us to embody the wilderness, we must choose how we *emerge from* the wilderness. Will we remember with gratitude how God led us and brought us through? Will we remember that He is the source of all our good gifts? Or will we forget the Lord and believe our blessings are the work of our own hands?

Moses advised the Israelites to watch out, taking care to never forget what they had seen, or the covenant God had made with them. He urged them to not allow their memories to be forgotten, implying that remembering requires intentional effort.

Stewarding the *land of milk*, or wilderness, is one type of challenge. Stewarding the *land of honey*—life outside the wilderness—is another. It's been astutely said that "the real challenge is not poverty but affluence, not slavery but freedom, not homelessness but home." In other words, the tests of the wilderness may not be the most difficult challenges we will face.

God-Dependence or Self-Dependence

One of the greatest gifts of a wilderness season is that it positions us to be dependent on God. He must intervene by way of provision, protection, guidance, comfort, healing—whatever our scenario requires.

In Deuteronomy 8, Moses repeatedly references God's work on the Israelites' behalf; their *God*-dependence through the wilderness and beyond. God brought them out of Egypt, the land of slavery. God led them through the wilderness, provided water from rock, and daily manna to eat. God was giving them a good land and bringing them into it.

Moses also warned of future blessings that could lull them into *self*-dependence, pride, and forgetfulness. The abundance of the Promised Land came with its own traps, chief of which was the potential to forget the Lord, when all was going well.

The danger is as real as ever today.

When we leave the wilderness or place of *God*-dependence, when we go to the farmland or place of potential *self*-dependence, we must beware of the temptation to forget the Lord our God.

Rhythms of Remembering

A rhythm of remembering what God has done, as well as where He has brought us from and to, is one of our most important practices for embodying the wilderness.

Deuteronomy 2 offers a comforting reminder that, as we *engage the process* by choosing to walk the wilderness path, the living God is mindful of each step and walking with us—just as He did for the Israelites. "For the LORD your God . . . has watched your every step through this great wilderness. During these forty years, the LORD your God has been with you, and you have lacked nothing" (v. 7 NLT).

All these years later, as we read of God providing the Israelites with daily manna, sandals and clothes that never wore out, water, and more, the vastness of divine intervention on their behalf may cause us to wonder how the Israelites could possibly forget. But when we take an honest look at ourselves, we will often see the propensity to forget God's work on *our* behalf. Rhythms of remembering help us proactively combat this inclination.

One of my primary rhythms of remembering is looking for opportunities to share my wilderness God-stories—experiences that remind me of my dependence on Him, and His movement on my behalf, during those long, difficult years. Stories that encourage others to watch for God at work in and through their wilderness seasons.

> I remember the "roses from heaven" I received three times as a thirty-year-old.

I remember the significant dreams God gave me when I wasn't seeing movement in my life. Through the quiet night hours, He spoke messages of affirmation, hope, and healing.

I remember the "hand of God" I saw in the clouds when prompted to *look up*.

I remember the recurrence of meaningful encounters happening on the same date for ten consecutive years.

I remember ongoing divine provision as I always had a place to live, clothes to wear, food to eat, and gas in my car.

I remember the miraculous way God got me back to Israel after a nearly eleven-year drought from the land.

I remember what's happened since that first trip "home," as I've had the opportunity to return multiple times, with more adventures on the horizon!

I remember words received in the wilderness that have come and are coming to pass.

When I share my wilderness God-stories, people often ask me how I remember dates, years, meaningful symbols, and moments with such clarity. I'm able to remember so well because of my rhythm of recording. When I see evidence of God moving on my behalf, I write it down. Sometimes I write a word or a sentence; other times several points or paragraphs—whatever the situation calls for. . . and I always include the date.

Towards the end of the year, I read back through my journal. This helps me recall with appreciation all God has done throughout the year. If I'm experiencing a low point, where my perspective needs to be adjusted, I'll pull out present and past journals to reread. Remembering helps me recalibrate. Remembering elicits gratitude.

A God Who Remembers

Let's pause to consider the word of the Lord to the Israelites, spoken through the prophet Jeremiah:

"I remember how eager you were to please me as a young bride long ago, how you loved me and followed me even through the barren wilderness. . . What did your ancestors find wrong with me that led them to stray so far from me?" (Jer. 2:2, 5 NLT)

The living God also *zakhars*; He remembers. When God *zakhars* the way we walk out our wilderness years and beyond, will He remember us as people who forgot Him and turned to "gods" such as our possessions and talents? Or will He remember us as people who continue to depend on and follow Him?

A Twelve-Stone Memorial

After years of waiting, the Israelites were finally headed into the Promised Land. The mantle of leadership had been passed from Moses to Joshua; a new era was beginning.

God allowed this generation to experience their own water story as the entire nation passed through the Jordan. Afterward, the Lord instructed Joshua to choose one man from each of the twelve tribes to take a stone from the middle of the Jordan where the priests were standing. They were to carry the stones with them and place them at their camp that night.

The twelve stones were intended to be a memorial sign for future generations; an opportunity to tell how the flow of the Jordan had been cut off before the ark of the covenant. In Hebrew, *zikrown* is the word for "memorial" and can also mean "reminder" or "remembrance." *Zikrown* may sound familiar, as it shares a root with *zakhar*, to remember.

Through this directive, God was helping the Israelites set up a rhythm of remembering by way of memorial stones that would be a conversation-starter for generations to come. As they shared their miraculous dry ground crossing of the Jordan before entering the Promised Land, that story would be a bridge for them to tell of their ancestors' miraculous crossing of the Red Sea after escaping from Egypt.

Celebration at Gilgal

Following forty years in the wilderness, Joshua, Caleb, and a new generation of Israelites arrived in the long-awaited Promised Land.

On the plains of Jericho at a place called Gilgal, the Israelites paused to remember by celebrating Passover. This festival was a way to collectively recall God's deliverance of the Israelites from the plague on the Egyptian firstborn, as well as their ensuing departure from Egypt.[4]

The *NIV First-Century Study Bible* offers unique perspective that "the second Passover preceded the Israelites' 'exodus' from the wilderness into the promised land." For the new generation who had not known the oppression of Egypt, "this sacred meal rooted their experience in the greater story of God's ongoing work of redemption, now experienced as liberation from the wilderness while reenacting in ritual form the exodus from Egypt."[5] Passover continues to be an annual rhythm of remembering for Jewish people, a community known for celebration.

Gilgal, the first place the Israelites camped in Canaan, sounds like the Hebrew word *galal*, meaning "to roll." After forty years in the wilderness, the Lord rolled away the reproach, or *shame*, of 430 years of bondage in Egypt. Reproach was not connected to their wilderness years; those were years of refining. The Israelites were a desert people, so they carried the wilderness with them always. For generation after generation, they would *embody the wilderness* by choosing to *zakhar* through ongoing rhythms of remembrance and celebration.

Some of the most pivotal words in the entire exodus-wilderness–Promised Land narrative, "the manna stopped" (Joshua 5:12) simultaneously communicates longing fulfilled and warning. The wilderness years were over; the Promised Land and the fruit it offered had finally been reached. The desire of a nation was being satisfied.

The familiar provisionary pattern of waking up to manna every morning, day after day, year after year, was over; the inclination to forget and exchange God-dependence for self-dependence was a real threat.

If we are not intentional to remember, we too will be a people who forget. We embody the wilderness by choosing a rhythm of remembering.

We are what we *zakhar*.

We are what we remember.

Zakhar the *midbar*; remember the wilderness.

Questions to Consider and *Yeshiva*

1. If you were to ask the people closest to you how you embody the wilderness, as well as what "wilderness residue" they see in or on you, what would they say?

2. Strap on the sandals of an Israelite. You've woken up in Canaan, and for the first time in forty years, there isn't manna on the ground to gather for your daily bread. Instead, the fruit of the land awaits. What are you thinking? How do you feel?

3. Describe your tendencies for self-dependence. What intentional rhythms keep you dependent on God?

4. The Israelites made a twelve-stone memorial so they could tell future generations about God's movement on their behalf. What type memorial will you shape to serve as a door-opener for sharing your wilderness God-stories?

5. What are your rhythms of remembering? Who do you remember with? What is your set-apart space or place for remembering?

12

EMERGE INTO A NEW SEASON

> There are three stages in a rite of passage.
> The first is separation, a symbolic break with the past . . .
> In between is the transition, the point at which the person . . .
> is remade, reconstituted, reborn. The third stage is
> re-incorporation, re-entering society with a new identity.
> —Rabbi Jonathan Sacks

When the Israelites experienced the change in diet from manna to unleavened bread and roasted grain, it was clear that a new day had dawned. After forty years of wilderness waiting, they emerged into a new season.

Chadash

The Hebrew word for "new" is *chadash*, which can also mean "new thing" or "fresh." For example:

> "See, I will create new [*chadash*] heavens and a new [*chadash*] earth" (Isa. 65:17).

> "I will give you a new [*chadash*] heart and put a new [*chadash*] spirit in you" (Ezek. 36:26).

In Isaiah 43:19, God says: "'See, I am doing a new thing [*chadash*]! Now it springs up; do you not perceive it? I am making a way in the wilderness and streams in the wasteland.'" This passage provides several keys for our tenth and final posture, *emerge into a new season*:

> *God* is doing the new thing; we don't have to make it happen.
>
> Our role is to *perceive* it; the new thing might not always be obvious.
>
> He is making a way *in* the wilderness; the new thing often begins in the liminal space.

This is where our senses that have been heightened through the wilderness—seeing and paying attention, hearing and responding—help us identify the "new" we are being led into. Because this often involves unfamiliar territory, we continue to walk the path before us, trusting each step to be a bridge on the journey.

Emerging

If we were to name all the scenarios in Scripture where a person or people group exited the wilderness and entered a promised land, we would come up with just one: the Israelites! Even then it was the generation born in the wilderness that inherited Canaan, the land flowing with milk and honey. A more accurate reality is that we emerge from the wilderness into a new season.

If we're still looking at wilderness through a Western lens, with an in-and-out approach, our tendency can be to hastily exit the wilderness, wanting to put as much distance between us and it as possible. Viewing wilderness through a Middle Eastern lens of function gives us a desire to *emerge from* or *arise out of* with gratitude for all God has done in and through our wilderness season, such as:

— inviting us to engage the process
— giving us eyes that see, ears that hear, and emotions to be expressed
— positioning us to encounter the divine
— summoning us to embrace the becoming

- strengthening us as we establish healthy rhythms
- encouraging us as we make the most of delays and detours
- challenging us to embody the wilderness

As we consider *chadash*, let's look at the new things God did for Hagar and the Hebrews, as well as the "new" we are being invited into.

Found

Years after Hagar and Ishmael were sent away, Sarah had died and Isaac, the son of promise, was wifeless—a significant issue if he were to continue the family line. Abraham saw the need and ever willing to join God and play an active role in the fulfillment of the covenant, sent his servant to find a wife for Isaac. He gave specific instructions that the woman must come from his own people, not the Canaanites.

God blessed the servant's search, and as he and Rebekah, the bride-to-be, were coming from her family's home in northwestern Mesopotamia, Isaac, who had been living in the Negev, was returning from Beer Lahai Roi (see Gen. 24:62).

You may recall that this location is first mentioned in Genesis 16, when pregnant Hagar, fleeing from Sarai into the wilderness, first encountered the angel of the Lord. The well where this meeting occurred was named Beer Lahai Roi, in keeping with the name Hagar gave God, *El Roi*.

Jewish tradition or *midrash* (rabbinic interpretation) holds that Isaac had gone to Beer Lahai Roi *in search of Hagar*. The formerly rejected maidservant was sought out by the covenant son, because once Isaac heard that his father was looking for a wife for him, he said, "'Shall I be married while my father lives alone? I will go and return Hagar to him.'"[1]

After Isaac and Rebekah married, the text tells us that "Abraham had taken another wife, whose name was Keturah" (Gen. 25:1). With so many details left out of the Torah's description of Abraham, it is interesting that his marriage *after* Sarah's death is mentioned, as well as the name of his new wife.

In Rabbi Sacks' compelling book *Not in God's Name*, he offers this explanation: "Who then was Keturah? Said the rabbis: Hagar herself!

Why then was she called Keturah? Because, said the sages, 'her acts were as fragrant as incense [*ketoret*].'"[2]

The Torah uses different names for Moses' father-in-law, referred to as both Reuel (Ex. 2:16-21) and Jethro (Ex. 3:1); so, it is not a stretch to consider that *Keturah* was indeed Hagar.

"The story beneath the story," continues Rabbi Sacks, "is that neither Abraham nor Isaac made their peace with the banishment of handmaid and child." We can now take a collective sigh of relief, as the sending away of Hagar and Ishmael, even when viewed through a Middle Eastern cultural lens, still doesn't feel fair. Rabbi Sacks' fascinating perspective goes on: "As long as Sarah was alive, they could do nothing about it, respecting her feelings as God had commanded Abraham to do. But once Sarah was no longer alive, they could engage in an act of reconciliation. That is how Isaac and Ishmael came to be together when Abraham died.[3]

Later in Genesis 25 we are told that after Abraham died, God blessed Isaac—who was then living near Beer Lahai Roi.

Location, location, location.

Regarding this, the midrash says: "Even after his father's death, Isaac lived near Hagar and treated her with respect."[4]

Hagar's *chadash*, after having been mistreated and abandoned, was being *found* by the Hebrew God in the wilderness. The new for her could have also included being sought out and *found* by Isaac for his father Abraham. This potential restorative ending certainly fits the redemptive thread woven all throughout the biblical narrative. It is quite representative of the Hebrew God's kindness toward Hagar, who may *not* have lived the rest of her days as a rejected outcast.

A New Thing

When we allow the wilderness to do its work, it yields a new thing in us. We've seen this reality in each of our wilderness narratives.

> The Israelites possessed the Promised Land as free people no longer weighed down by the reproach of slavery.

> Moses emerged from forty years in Midian as a prophet, deliverer, and leader who relied on God more than himself.

Elijah left Horeb with much-needed renewal to finish strong in his prophetic mantle.

David's dependence on and desire for God were cultivated through years of shepherding and seeking refuge in the wilderness.

Jesus emerged from the wilderness with His *halakha*, as well as an unflinching resolve that would carry Him to the cross.

March 18

I'll never forget the sequence of moments that ushered me into a new season.

To string some pearls from my story, when I was thirty years old, I had a life-altering experience on March 18. Another such encounter followed on March 18 the next year . . . and the next. Year after year, March 18 brought unique happenings that radically shifted my internal life and gave me hope that God saw me in my wilderness.

Fast-forward to the latter part of 2017, when I was given an itinerary for a spring 2018 Israel trip. I noticed that the team was scheduled to be in the *Judean wilderness*—where I had hiked at the onset of my eleven-year wilderness season—on *March 18, 2018*! Even though this trip was filled to capacity, and I had no extra money to put toward it, I began "faith-ing" for the adventure that had found me.

Over the next few months, I continued walking the path before me, including updating my passport so I would be prepared *when* the time came to return to Israel. In February, I wrote: *God is looking for a people that will actively participate in His promise . . . what He is doing.* I wanted to *faith* the way men and women in the Bible had.

Just three days before take-off in early March, through a whirlwind of generosity and closed doors opening, I had a ticket to Israel and a spot on the team. I was headed "home" for the first time in over a decade and could not have been more thrilled!

Going Home

The timing, the team, the land . . . everything about my return experience was surreal! Some sights, sounds, and smells were familiar; others were new. I breathed deeply and took it all in, grateful to be back.

March 18, 2018 began with a beautiful sunrise overlooking the Sea of Galilee, accompanied by a force of wind I'd not previously experienced in the land. The Hebrews believe that when the wind—or *ruach*—is blowing, the Spirit—or *Ruach*—is moving, a belief that compels them to ask, "What are you doing in me today, Holy Spirit?"

One of our early sites of the day was Dan, in the northernmost region of Israel. As we headed toward the hiking path, I paused to take a closer look at a spring of flowing water. Then and there, with the wind still blowing, I heard the life-giving words of Isaiah 58:

> The Lord will guide you always; he will satisfy your needs in a sun-scorched land and will strengthen your frame. You will be like a well-watered garden, like a spring whose waters never fail. You will rebuild the ancient ruins; you will restore the foundations laid long ago; you will be called the repairer of broken walls, the restorer of streets where people live. (11-12 NIV, HCSB)

As I watched the rapidly flowing waters and received this *davar*, I knew I was emerging from the eleven-year wilderness season. The living God had indeed led me and satisfied each of my needs in the "sun-scorched land" known as wilderness. He was naming my future, as He had done for Hagar, Moses, and Elijah.

The wind followed us throughout the day, a tangible reminder of the Spirit's movement among us. March 18, 2018 culminated with a brilliant sunset above the Sea of Galilee. My heart was full.

Why March 18?

After several years of March 18 God-encounters, I wondered, *Why March 18? Why has this been the date God keeps choosing to speak to me in such unique and profound ways?* Then I recalled that my first time flying to Israel had been on March 19—a date etched in my memory as representing a dream ending prematurely, ushering me into an eleven-year wilderness season. Through March 18, God was graciously reshaping what I would remember; a new date that carried life and promise.

Restitution

For as seemingly never-ending as my wilderness season was, when I emerged, it was all I could do to keep up with the "suddenly" I had been thrust into. *Chadash*, the "new thing," for me has been *restitution*: God giving back far more than was ever lost.

Following a nearly eleven-year "drought" from Israel, I studied in the land for a month in 2018 and six weeks in 2019—including being there again on March 18! Even with eyes that see, I never saw that coming.

Isaiah 58:11–12 now hangs on a large sign above my couch, visible to everyone who walks through my front door. It is a continual reminder to *zakhar* my *midbar*; to remember my wilderness, and God's faithfulness through it.

Finding God in Disappointment

As March 18, 2020, approached, my expectancy was high. I was forty, and it felt as though this ten-year marker date was going to bookend what had begun at thirty.

I was scheduled to be in Israel and Egypt for a month, exploring southern Israeli wilderness regions with desert archeologist Dr. Uzi Avner on March 18, before heading on to Egypt and the Sinai. This felt significant to experience while being forty, as Moses and Elijah had encountered God at Horeb (Sinai), and "forty" was present in both their narratives.

But as happened for so many, the coronavirus pandemic halted my travel plans. When March 18 arrived, though disappointed at not being in the Middle East, my eyes were open, watching for what God was doing. I looked and looked, but for the first time in ten years, I saw nothing. The nothingness hit me hard.

My travel agent called the next day, March 19, to rebook my flight to Israel. She said I was receiving a credit, as this new flight was slightly less than the original. Tears filled my eyes as I saw the credit amount: *$318.40*—a combination of the date that has been so significant for me (3/18) and my age (40)!

What I "saw" in that moment was God bridging my heart back to March 19, restoring the date I had for years remembered with a sense of loss. Even in disappointment, there was purpose and redemption.

Always in Proximity

One of the geographical certainties of Israel is that when in the land, we are always in proximity to a wilderness—whether that be the Judean, Negev, Sinai, Arabian, or Sahara. Some desert region is just over the horizon, and likely behind or on either side of us as well.

The same is true in life: we are always close to a wilderness season by way of being in one, emerging from one, or heading into one. This reality affirms the importance of actively choosing postures that position us to receive the wealth God has for us in and through wilderness seasons.

Unexpected Grief

While excitement at the thought of a wilderness season coming to an end may seem like the normal response, there may be an unexpected grief that accompanies it. The Torah does not explicitly tell us, but the children of Israel might have experienced a measure of sorrow when, upon eating the fruit of Canaan, the daily provision of manna came to a sudden halt.

As we emerge into a new season, there needs to be space for all types of emotions to be felt and expressed: gratitude, expectation, relief, fear of the unknown, sadness. Emerging will feel different for each of us.

Each time I come out of the Wilderness of Zin, the Negev, or the Judean wilderness, I experience both exhilaration and deep sadness. It's as though I'm walking out of unique space that feels like home. When I'm not in the wilderness, I miss it. I think about it. I long to return. No other place matches its allure and mystique. The wilderness simultaneously beckons and repels. It is deep calling to deep.

Wilderness residue has a way of getting on you and staying in you for life . . . long after your sweat-streaked, sandy hiking clothes have been washed and put away.

Everything Will Be New

As I write this section, I am sitting on a balcony overlooking the Sea of Galilee. A gentle breeze invites a calm that reaches deep into my soul. The twinkling lights of Tiberias are visible on the opposite shore, with a soft pink sunset providing a beautiful backdrop.

The Galilee is in northern Israel, with lush green topography that starkly contrasts the barren, dry terrain of the southern wilderness regions. Jesus was known as a rabbi of the north; He performed ninety percent of His earthly ministry here.

Most, if not all, who needed a miraculous, healing touch from Jesus were experiencing a circumstantial wilderness:

— the man who had been lame for thirty-eight years
— the woman with the twelve-year issue of blood
— the man blind from birth
— demoniacs
— Mary and Martha, as they mourned the death of their brother, Lazarus

and countless others. While the Galilean landscape looks, sounds, smells, and feels drastically different from Israeli deserts, the reality of wilderness *seasons* is present and felt all throughout the land—just as it is in our lives.

From this balcony, I am positioned up higher, with a view of the very sea where Jesus called His disciples and demonstrated mastery over the chaos by walking on water and speaking peace to the wind and waves.

As I enjoy the calming view, I can't help but think of families who have recently entered severe wilderness seasons, their lives forever altered as they wake up into new, unwelcome normals. Others have already been weathering a wilderness and are facing the intensified heat and weariness that often comes with extended duration. Some are not yet aware of the wilderness on their horizon, just as the fading sun sits above the mountains across the seashore. Wilderness comes in all forms, and it comes for all of us.

Looking out on this body of water that is void of recreational boats, I am reminded that even today, the land of the Bible is still the land of desert people. It's their familiar, though that certainly doesn't imply that wilderness is easy for Middle Easterners.

With the Sea of Galilee ever in my line of vision, I've had ample time today to implement my *rhythm of release*, logging miles of walking, looking, and listening. Step after step, I've asked God for eyes that see and ears that hear. In doing so, my thoughts have been directed to Revelation 21 and the vision given to the apostle John in the latter years of his life. We might say John was in a wilderness season, exiled on the island of Patmos, when he encountered the divine.

John writes: "Then I saw a new heaven and a new earth, for the old heaven and the old earth had disappeared. And the sea was also gone" (v. 1 NLT). As a Hebrew in the ancient Near Eastern world who walked with and learned from Jesus, John would have understood this vision of things to come was a new heaven and earth where calm will replace chaos and *shalom* (peace and tranquility) will replace the abyss.

John's vision continues: "I heard a loud voice from the throne saying, 'Look! God's dwelling place is now among the people, and he will dwell with them. They will be his people, and God himself will be with them and be their God'" (v. 3). In the wilderness, God traveled with and among the people in the *mishkan*, or tabernacle; His temporary tent that resembled their temporary tents. In the new heaven and earth, God will again make His home among the people—but this time, it will be a *permanent* home.

And there will be no more death, sorrow, crying, or pain. The living God is making all things new, a promise we can anticipate and look forward to!

Until that time, *Wealth of the Wilderness* offers us postures for walking and living that position us to inherit the riches God has for us in and through the wilderness seasons we are certain to experience. May we choose to be desert people who

> run *to* the wilderness instead of running *from* it
>
> position ourselves to thrive instead of merely survive
>
> allow the wilderness to transform those parts of us that need to change
>
> yield to this unique space that transitions us from one phase of life to another
>
> *zakhar* the *midbar*—remember the wilderness—by sharing our God-stories with others.

EMERGE INTO A NEW SEASON

Regarding the Israelites' journey through the wilderness, historian Eric Voegelin once said: "The desert was only a station on the way, not the goal; for in the desert the tribes found their God."[5]

The same can be true for us. In the wilderness, we can find our God.

May we courage into taking the next step on this transformational pathway.

Questions to Consider and *Yeshiva*

1. What new thing do you perceive God doing in and through your wilderness? How does this give you hope to keep walking the path before you?

2. How has your posture toward wilderness seasons shifted as you have discovered potential functions or purposes of challenging times?

3. As you consider the unexpected grief that may accompany emerging into a new season, what about your wilderness experience might you miss?

4. "You haven't learned a thing when you've seen it, and you haven't learned a thing when you've heard it. You haven't learned a thing when you've seen *and* heard it," Kristi McLelland often tells her students. "You've learned a thing when you can give it away."[6]

   With whom in your sphere of influence will you "give away" what you have learned through *Wealth of the Wilderness*?

ACKNOWLEDGMENTS

Wealth of the Wilderness has been and will continue to be a communal effort. My gratitude runs deep for:

>those who have journeyed through a *Wealth of the Wilderness* transformational table. Your curiosity, questions, and feedback have been vital in shaping this work.
>
>all who have prayed, encouraged, and generously given, allowing me to return to Israel more than I ever anticipated and affording me time to research and write.
>
>Tamera Alexander, for your confidence in me and this message; for your advice and kindhearted enthusiasm in moving it forward.
>
>Dr. Gabi Barkay, for allowing me to learn from you at archeological sites in Israel and around dinner tables in the States.
>
>Dr. Uzi Avner, for graciously answering my questions and open-handedly sharing your wilderness expertise.
>
>my sister Jenni, for a lifetime of shared experiences: first as playmates and roommates; then as teammates and student-athletes; now as allies, lifelong growers, and so much more! You are a gift to me and this world.
>
>Kristi, for believing in me from the beginning; for being my *haver* and bridge back "home" to the Land that continues to summon and shape us. I smile when I think about us being wrecked by Israel for the first time the *same* year, though we would not meet for another decade.

GLOSSARY

Avodah (a-vod-ah). Hard work or labor; to serve; worship.

Bamidbar (bah-mid-BAR). "In the wilderness." The Hebrew name for the book of Numbers.

Chadash (KHA-dash). New, new thing, fresh.

Davar (duh-var). Word. Speaking, speech. Saying. Thing.

Essenes. One of the four most influential reform groups—along with the Pharisees, Sadducees, and Zealots—during the time of Christ. They opposed the pagan influences that threatened to corrupt Judaism. They chose a communal, purist lifestyle in the Judean wilderness.

Halakh (ha-LAKH; lit., "walk"). To come. To go.

Halakha (hal-a-KHA). A way of walking or living.

Haver (ha-VAIR; lit., "friend"). Comrade, companion.

Lev (lave). Heart. Inner man, mind, will, understanding. Seat of emotions and passions. Conscience.

Midbar (mid-BAR). A desert or wilderness where human habitation is difficult.

Midrash (mi-DRASH or MIH-drash). Rabbinic explanation and commentary on the biblical text; can also refer to a collection of commentaries on the Scriptures.

Mishkan (mish-KHON). Tabernacle or dwelling place.

Mishnah (mish-NAH or MISH-nah). A collection of rabbinic rulings and sayings gathered and put into writing around AD 200.

Ra'ah (ra-AH). To intentionally see. To look at, inspect, perceive, consider, discern.

Remez (RI-mez). Hint. A Jewish explanatory method used for typological or allegorical interpretations of Scripture.

Sabab (suh-VAV). To go around. To turn about. Roundabout.

Shabbat (shah-BAHT). Hebrew for "Sabbath," which means "to cease." Jews observe Shabbat from Friday sunset to Saturday sunset.

Shakach (shuh-KAKH). To forget or ignore. To cease to care.

Shema (she-MAH; lit., "hear"). Implies listening followed by action; an obedient response.

Shulhan (shool-KHAN). Table. Originates from the ancient belief that table fellowship, or eating at a table with others, is the foundation of a peaceful, harmonious relationship.

Talmud (TAHL-mood). A large volume of commentary on the Mishnah, printed section by section after each verse of the Mishnah. The Jerusalem Talmud was completed around AD 400 and the Babylonian Talmud, which is considered authoritative by Jews today, was completed around AD 500.

Tanakh (TAH-nakh or tah-NAHK). The Jewish term for the Bible; includes all the books of the Protestant Old Testament. *Tanakh* is an acronym for the first letters of its three primary sections:

Torah (TOR-ah). The five books of Moses; covenant and laws.
Neviim (neh-vee-YEEM). lit., "prophets."
Ketuvim (ket-u-VEEM). lit., "writings."

Torah (TOR-ah). Meaning "teaching" or "instruction;" refers to the first five books of the Bible, also called the Pentateuch.

Yeshiva (yeh-SHEEV-ah). As a noun, *yeshiva* is a Jewish school or college where students study religious texts, such as the Torah and Talmud. As a verb, to *yeshiva* can imply discovering, learning, and pondering the Scriptures together.

Zakhar (zuh-KHAR). To remember, recall, call to mind.

NOTES

Preface

1. Dr. Edith Eva Eger, *The Choice* (New York: Scribner, 2017), 48.

Chapter 1: *Which Lens Are You Looking Through?*

1. Lois Tverberg, *Reading the Bible with Rabbi Jesus* (Grand Rapids: Baker Books, 2017), 34.
2. Tverberg, 136.
3. Tverberg, 136.
4. Miriam Rodlyn Park, *Watchmen on the Wall: A Practical Guide to Prayer for Jerusalem* (Clarence, NY: Kairos, 2005).
5. Kristi McLelland, *Jesus and Women*, Session 3, 24:00, https://www.lifeway.com/jesusandwomen.
6. *NIV First-Century Study Bible* (Grand Rapids: Zondervan, 2014), 1574.
7. Ursula K. Le Guin, *The Left Hand of Darkness* (New York: Ace, 1987), 237.
8. Levison Wood, *An Arabian Journey* (New York: Atlantic Monthly Press, 2019), 153.
9. Lois Tverberg, *Sitting at the Feet of Rabbi Jesus* (Grand Rapids: Zondervan, 2009), 231.

Chapter 2: *What Is the Wilderness?*

1. Jonathan Sacks, *Numbers: The Wilderness Years* (Jerusalem: Maggid Books, 2017), 15.
2. Richard Rohr, *Adam's Return* (New York: Crossroad, 2004), 135-138.
3. Brené Brown, "Brené on Day 2," Unlocking Us—September 2, 2020, podcast, 6:21, https://brenebrown.com/podcast/brene-on-day-2/.
4. Lois Tverberg, *Walking in the Dust of Rabbi Jesus* (Grand Rapids: Zondervan, 2012), 36-37.
5. Rob Bell, *Sex God* (San Francisco: HarperOne, 2012), 51.
6. *NIV Archaeological Study Bible* (Grand Rapids: Zondervan, 2005), 34.
7. Sacks, *Numbers*, 43.
8. Thomas Cahill, *The Gifts of the Jews* (New York: Doubleday, 1998), 161.

Chapter 3: *Engage the Process*

1. Jonathan Sacks, "Rabbi Lord Jonathan Sacks: Life Worth Living and the Jewish Tradition," Yale Center for Faith and Culture, March 27, 2015, YouTube video, 40:54, https://www.youtube.com/watch?v=bWpQ-23OBtU.
2. Nabeel Qureshi, *Seeking Allah, Finding Jesus* (Grand Rapids: Zondervan, 2016), 59.

3. C. S. Lewis, *The Lion, the Witch and the Wardrobe* (New York: Scholastic, 1950), 184.
4. John C. Maxwell, *The 15 Invaluable Laws of Growth* (New York: Hachette, 2012), 121.
5. Sacks, *Numbers*, 3 (see chap. 2, n. 1).
6. *NIV Cultural Backgrounds Study Bible* (Grand Rapids: Zondervan, 2016), 605.
7. Cahill, *The Gifts of the Jews*, 132–33 (see chap. 2, n. 8).
8. Kristi McLelland, *Israel*, Week 8, 14:25, https://newlensbiblicalstudies.teachable.com/p/israel.
9. McLelland, *Israel*, Week 8, 43:55.
10. Geza Vermes, *The Complete Dead Sea Scrolls* (New York: Penguin Books, 1998), 1QS VIII, 12–15.
11. Josephus, *The Jewish War* (London: Penguin Books, 1959), 133.
12. Ravi Zacharias, Who Are You God? Part 2 of 4, August 29, 2017, https://www.rzim.org/listen/just-thinking/who-are-you-god-part-2-of-4
13. Henri J. M. Nouwen, *The Way of the Heart* (New York: Seabury, 1981), 14.
14. Thomas Merton, *The Wisdom of the Desert* (New York: New Directions, 1960), 3.
15. Nouwen, *The Way of the Heart*, 24.

Chapter 4: *Develop Eyes that See*

1. Barbara Brown Taylor, *Learning to Walk in the Dark* (New York: HarperCollins, 2014), 106.
2. Peter M. Leschak, quoted in Maxwell, *The 15 Invaluable Laws of Growth*, 58 (see chap. 3, n. 4).
3. *NIV Cultural Backgrounds Study Bible*, 109 (see chap. 3, n. 6).
4. *NIV Archaeological Study Bible*, 28 (see chap. 2, n. 6).
5. *NIV Cultural Backgrounds Study Bible*, 1416.
6. James L. Kugel, *Traditions of the Bible* (Cambridge: Harvard University Press, 1998), 530.
7. *NIV First-Century Study Bible*, 85 (see chap. 1, n. 6).
8. Cahill, *The Gifts of the Jews*, 104–5 (see chap. 2, n. 8).
9. Rabbi Moshe David Cassuto, *A Commentary on the Book of Exodus* (Jerusalem: Magnes Press, Hebrew University, 1967).
10. W. David Nelson, *Mekhilta de-Rabbi Shimon bar Yohai* (Philadelphia: Jewish Publication Society, 2006), Tractate Sanya, 1:1.
11. Jacob Neusner, *The Babylonian Talmud* (n.p.: Hendrickson, 2011), b. *Shabbat* 6:9, l. 13. A–C.
12. Barbara Brown Taylor, *An Altar in the World* (New York: HarperCollins, 2010), 25.
13. Liora Ravid, *Daily Life in Biblical Times* (Jerusalem: Gefen, 2013), 120–21.
14. Ravid, 4.
15. Sharon Pace Jeansonne, *The Women of Genesis* (Minneapolis: Fortress Press, 1990), 19.
16. *NIV Cultural Backgrounds Study Bible*, 44.

Chapter 5: *Cultivate Ears that Hear*

1. Jonathan Sacks, *Deuteronomy: Renewal of the Sinai Covenant* (Jerusalem: Maggid Books, 2019), 67.
2. *NIV Cultural Backgrounds Study Bible*, 606 (see chap. 3, n. 6).

3. Jonathan Sacks, "The Sound of Silence (Bamidbar 5776)," The Office of Rabbi Sacks, May 31, 2016, http://rabbisacks.org/sound-silence-bamidbar-5776/.
4. Heinrich Graetz, "Judaism Can Be Understood Only Through Its History," in *Ideas of Jewish History*, ed. Michael Meyer (New York: Behrman House, 1974), 223.
5. Tverberg, *Walking in the Dust of Rabbi Jesus*, 118 (see chap. 2, n. 4).
6. Sacks, *Numbers*, 49-50 (see chap. 2, n. 1).

Chapter 6: *Express Authentic Emotions*

1. Brené Brown, *Braving the Wilderness* (New York: Random House, 2017), 36.

Chapter 7: *Perceive Encounters with the Divine*

1. *NIV Cultural Backgrounds Study Bible*, 109 (see chap. 3, n. 6).
2. Jonathan Sacks, YouTube video, 12:40 (see chap. 3, n. 1).
3. Jonathan Sacks, *Exodus: The Book of Redemption* (Jerusalem: Maggid Books, 2010), 52.
4. Tverberg, *Reading the Bible with Rabbi Jesus*, 260 (see chap. 1, n. 1).
5. *NIV First-Century Study Bible*, 104 (see chap. 1, n. 6).
6. Nahum Sarna, *The JPS Torah Commentary: Exodus* (Philadelphia: Jewish Publication Society, 1991).
7. Sacks, *Numbers*, 54 (see chap. 2, n. 1).

Chapter 8: *Embrace the Becoming*

1. Sue Monk Kidd, "Brené with Sue Monk Kidd and Jen Hatmaker on Longing, Belonging and Faith," Unlocking Us—April 28, 2020, podcast, 17:13, https://brenebrown.com/podcast/brene-with-sue-monk-kidd-and-jen-hatmaker-on-longing-belonging-and-faith/.
2. James Allen, *As a Man Thinketh*, 4th ed. (Chicago: Sheldon University Press, 1908), 22.
3. Sacks, *Numbers*, 3 (see chap. 2, n. 1).
4. Cahill, *The Gifts of the Jews*, 107 (see chap. 2, n. 8).
5. Cahill, 107.
6. McLelland, *Israel*, Week 3, 1:14:52 (see chap. 3, n. 8).
7. Sacks, *Numbers*, 11–12 (see chap. 2, n. 1).
8. Cahill, *The Gifts of the Jews*, 159–60.
9. Sacks, *Numbers*, 42–43.
10. Hannah Hurnard, *Hinds' Feet on High Places* (Wheaton, IL: Living Books, 1975), 126.

Chapter 9: *Establish Healthy Rhythms*

1. Maxwell, *The 15 Invaluable Laws of Growth*, 73 (see chap. 3, n. 4).
2. Kristi McLelland, *Sabbath*, Week 1, 59:34, https://newlensbiblicalstudies.teachable.com/p/sabbath.
3. Abraham Joshua Heschel, *The Sabbath* (New York: Farrar, Straus and Giroux, 1951), xiv.
4. Heschel, xv.
5. Cahill, *The Gifts of the Jews*, 144 (see chap. 2, n. 8).
6. Sacks, *Exodus*, 261–62 (see chap. 7, n. 3).

7. Barbara Brown Taylor, *Leaving Church*, (New York: HarperCollins, 2006), 136.
8. *NIV First-Century Study Bible*, 1198 (see chap. 1, n. 6).
9. Taylor, *An Alter in the World*, 66 (see chap. 4, n. 13).
10. Maxwell, *The 15 Invaluable Laws of Growth*, 93.
11. Quoted in Maxwell, 91.
12. Henry Cloud, *The Power of the Other* (New York: HarperCollins, 2016), 9.
13. Taylor, *An Alter in the World*, 56.
14. Simon Dubnow, quoted in "Rabbi Lord Jonathan Sacks: The World We Make With Words," Jewish Broadcasting Service, April 21, 2016, YouTube video, 7:19, https://www.youtube.com/watch?v=CNcel77Agbw.

Chapter 10: *Make the Most of Delays and Detours*

1. Eger, *The Choice*, 157 (see preface, n. 1).
2. Cahill, *The Gifts of the Jews*, 118 (see chap. 2, n. 8).
3. Moses Maimonides, *The Guide for the Perplexed* (London: George Routledge & Sons Ltd, 1919), III:32.
4. Jonathan Sacks, "Jonathan Sacks and Richards Dawkins at BBC RE:Think Festival," Brian Sacks, September 12, 2012, YouTube video, 16:18, https://m.youtube.com/watch?feature=youtu.be&v=roFdPHdhgKQ.
5. McLelland, *Israel*, Week 3, (see chap. 3, n. 8).
6. Ravid, *Daily Life in Biblical Times*, 176 (see chap. 4, n. 13).
7. *NIV Cultural Backgrounds Study Bible*, 59 (see chap. 3, n. 6).
8. Victor Frankl, *Man's Search for Meaning* (Boston: Beacon Press, 2006), 112.

Chapter 11: *Embody the Wilderness*

1. Tverberg, *Reading the Bible with Rabbi Jesus*, 73 (see chap. 1, n. 1).
2. Sacks, *Deuteronomy*, 223 (see chap. 5, n. 1).
3. Ray Vander Laan, "Understanding Green Pastures | Shepherd Lesson | Psalm 23," Life Lessons, May 28, 2017, YouTube video, 1:11, https://www.youtube.com/watch?v=2x8MwiTs0hM.
4. *NIV Archaeological Study Bible*, 656 (see chap. 2, n. 6).
5. *NIV First-Century Study Bible*, 286.

Chapter 12: *Emerge into a New Season*

1. *Bereshit Raba* 60:14
2. Jonathan Sacks, *Not in God's Name* (New York: Schocken, 2015), 121.
3. Sacks, *Not in God's Name*, 121.
4. Jonathan Sacks, "Isaac and Esau (Toldot 5780)," The Office of Rabbi Sacks—November 26, 2019, podcast, 6:10, https://rabbisacks.org/isaac-and-eisav-toldot-5780/.
5. Eric Voegelin, *Israel and Revelation*, vol. 1 of *Order and History* (Baton Rouge: Louisiana State University Press, 1956), 153.
6. McLelland, *Israel*, Week 5, 0:39 (see chap. 3, n. 8).

ADDITIONAL RESOURCES

- Bell, Rob. *What is the Bible? How an Ancient Library of Poems, Letters, and Stories Can Transform the Way You Think and Feel About Everything.* San Francisco: HarperOne, 2019.
- Cahill, Thomas. *The Gifts of the Jews: How a Tribe of Desert Nomads Changed the Way Everyone Thinks and Feels.* New York: Doubleday, 1998.
- Eger, Dr. Edith Eva. *The Choice: Embrace the Possible.* New York: Scribner, 2017.
- Hurnard, Hannah. *Hinds' Feet on High Places.* Wheaton: Living Books, 1975.
- Maxwell, John C. *The 15 Invaluable Laws of Growth: Live Them and Reach Your Potential.* New York: Hachette, 2012.
- McLelland, Kristi. *Israel Series.* https://newlensbiblicalstudies.teachable.com/p/israel.
- McLelland, Kristi. *Jesus and Women.* https://www.lifeway.com/jesusandwomen.
- McLelland, Kristi. *Sabbath Series.* https://newlensbiblicalstudies.teachable.com/p/sabbath.
- *NIV Archaeological Study Bible: An Illustrated Walk Through Biblical History and Culture.* Grand Rapids: Zondervan, 2006.
- *NIV Cultural Backgrounds Study Bible: Bringing to Life the Ancient World of Scripture.* Grand Rapids: Zondervan, 2016.
- *NIV First-Century Study Bible: Explore Scripture in its Jewish and Early Christian Context.* Grand Rapids: Zondervan, 2014.
- Ravid, Liora. *Daily Life in Biblical Times.* Jerusalem: Gefen, 2013.

- Richard, E. Randolph, and Brandon J. O'Brien. *Misreading Scripture with Western Eyes: Removing Cultural Blinders to Better Understand the Bible*. Downers Grove: InterVarsity Press, 2012.
- Sacks, Jonathan. *Deuteronomy: Renewal of the Sinai Covenant*. Jerusalem: Maggid Books, 2019.
- Sacks, Jonathan. *Exodus: The Book of Redemption*. Jerusalem: Maggid Books, 2010.
- Sacks, Jonathan. *Genesis: The Book of Beginnings*. Jerusalem: Maggid Books, 2009.
- Sacks, Jonathan. *Leviticus: The Book of Holiness*. Jerusalem: Maggid Books, 2015.
- Sacks, Jonathan. *Life Worth Living*. Yale Center for Faith and Culture: YouTube, 2015.
- Sacks, Jonathan. *Not in God's Name: Confronting Religious Violence*. New York: Schocken, 2015.
- Sacks, Jonathan. *Numbers: The Wilderness Years*. Jerusalem: Maggid Books, 2017.
- Spangler, Ann, and Lois Tverberg. *Sitting at the Feet of Rabbi Jesus: How the Jewishness of Jesus Can Transform Your Faith*. Grand Rapids: Zondervan, 2009.
- Taylor, Barbara Brown. *An Altar in the World*. New York: HarperCollins, 2010.
- Taylor, Barbara Brown. *Learning to Walk in the Dark*. New York: HarperCollins, 2014.
- Tverberg, Lois. *Reading the Bible with Rabbi Jesus: How a Jewish Perspective Can Transform Your Understanding*. Grand Rapids: Baker Books, 2017.
- Tverberg, Lois. *Walking in the Dust of Rabbi Jesus: How the Jewish Words of Jesus Can Change Your Life*. Grand Rapids: Zondervan, 2012.
- Wood, Levison. *An Arabian Journey: One Man's Quest Through the Heart of the Middle East*. New York: Atlantic Monthly Press, 2019.

ABOUT THE COVER

The background pictures on the front and back cover were taken during my first hike through the Judean wilderness. The bright red flower on the front flap was the only pop of color I saw amidst the barren landscape.

On the inside front cover:

The background pictures are from my first hike through the Judean wilderness.

A Bedouin family's goats are grazing on wilderness patches of green that aptly represent the "green pastures" mentioned by the Psalmist.

Encountering a narrowing path above a cliff face while hiking through the Judean wilderness is noted on page 9.

A shepherd crossing the street with his sheep in Bethlehem is referenced on page 5.

The story behind the red rose with sticky note is shared on pages 90–91.

The "Hand of God in the sky" is detailed on page 48.

The pictures on the back cover capture my return trips to Israel after a nearly eleven-year "drought" from the land.

Under the title, I am pictured at Maktesh Ramon in the Negev desert of southern Israel.

Beneath my bio on the back flap, the Wilderness of Zin is the landscape behind me.

On the inside back cover:

The background pictures were taken at En Gedi, a natural oasis in the Judean wilderness. Big thanks to Grace Kerrington for capturing me in a type of desert baptism under this beautiful waterfall, as well as hiking with my friend Kristi through this wilderness haven.

My sister Jenni and I are pictured in a *wadi* as we trekked through the Wilderness of Zin.

I'm with my friends Tiffini (center) and Kristi (right) after hiking through and out of Zin.

The story behind March 18, 2018 and sunset over the Sea of Galilee is told on pages 145–146.